ALICE DREAMING
A Play for Secondary Students

Ned Manning

Shaftesbury Road, Cambridge CB2 8EA, United Kingdom

One Liberty Plaza, 20th Floor, New York, NY 10006, USA

477 Williamstown Road, Port Melbourne, VIC 3207, Australia

314–321, 3rd Floor, Plot 3, Splendor Forum, Jasola District Centre, New Delhi – 110025, India

103 Penang Road, #05–06/07, Visioncrest Commercial, Singapore 238467

Cambridge University Press is part of the University of Cambridge.

We share the University's mission to contribute to society through the pursuit of education, learning and research at the highest international levels of excellence.

www.cambridge.org
Information on this title: www.cambridge.org/9780521166263

© Ned Manning 2010

This publication is in copyright. Subject to statutory exception and to the provisions of relevant collective licensing agreements, no reproduction of any part may take place without the written permission of Cambridge University Press.

First published 2010
Reprinted 2014

Typeset, illustrations and design by Sardine Design

A Cataloguing-in-Publication entry is available from the catalogue of the National Library of Australia at www.nla.gov.au

ISBN   978-0-521-16626-3   Paperback

Reproduction and communication for educational purposes
The Australian *Copyright Act 1968* (the Act) allows a maximum of one chapter or 10% of the pages of this publication, whichever is the greater, to be reproduced and/or communicated by any educational institution for its educational purposes provided that the educational institution (or the body that administers it) has given a remuneration notice to Copyright Agency Limited (CAL) under the Act.

For details of the CAL licence for educational institutions contact:
Copyright Agency Limited

Level 15, 233 Castlereagh Street
Sydney NSW 2000
Telephone: (02) 9394 7600
Facsimile: (02) 9394 7601
Email: info@copyright.com.au

Reproduction and communication for other purposes
Except as permitted under the Act (for example a fair dealing for the purposes of study, research, criticism or review) no part of this publication may be reproduced, stored in a retrieval system, communicated or transmitted in any form or by any means without prior written permission. All inquiries should be made to the publisher at the address above.

Cambridge University Press has no responsibility for the persistence or accuracy of URLs for external or third-party internet websites referred to in this publication, and does not guarantee that any content on such websites is, or will remain, accurate or appropriate. Information regarding prices, travel timetables, and other factual information given in this work is correct at the time of first printing but Cambridge University Press does not guarantee the accuracy of such information thereafter.

....

NOTICE TO TEACHERS
The photocopy masters in this publication may be photocopied or distributed [electronically] free of charge for classroom use within the school or institution that purchased the publication. Worksheets and copies of them remain in the copyright of Cambridge University Press, and such copies may not be distributed or used in any way outside the purchasing institution.

contents

ii   About Ned Manning

iii   Introduction by the playwright

iv   List of characters

v   Original production notes

3   The play and lesson plans

about Ned Manning

Ned Manning is a teacher, playwright and actor. He has been the recipient of the NSW Premiers Award and a Senior Examiner in HSC Drama. He has taught drama at Newtown High School of the Performing Arts and the EORA Centre in Redfern.

Ned's plays have been performed throughout Australia and overseas. He has written Bell Shakespeare's *Actors at Work* plays since 2005 and has also written a number of large cast plays for schools. Other plays such as *Luck of the Draw* and *Close to the Bone* demonstrate a strong concern with Australian and Indigenous themes. As an actor, Ned has worked extensively in theatre, television and film, including the cult classic *Dead End Drive-In* and *Looking for Alibrandi*.

introduction by the playwright

The idea of a journey has been at the heart of story telling from the beginning of time. *Alice Dreaming* is a story about a teenage girl's journey from introspection to the kind of extroversion that might be seen as a typical part of the Australian character. Alice becomes the kind of 'can do' girl the Prime Minister referred to in his Australia Day address in 2010. She might even go on to become the Young Australian of the Year in 2020!

Inspired by *Alice's Adventures in Wonderland* by Lewis Carroll and *The Wizard of Oz* by L. Frank Baum, it is a coming of age story aimed at teenagers and for teenagers.

It seems to me that sometimes the world of a teenager can be very inward looking. This is, of course, perfectly natural given all the social pressures on teenagers today. I wondered what would happen if someone was suddenly, magically, transported out of the security of their own world into the world at large. How would they react? What would they encounter?

I wanted to give Alice a 'bird's eye view' of some of the things that might affect the way she sees the world: entrapment, friendship, body image, communication and her sense of belonging.

I also wanted to see what she made of *my* world, the adult world.

Most importantly I wanted this play to be fun to read and perform. I have deliberately written it in a style that is open to many interpretations.

You can do it with a cast of 30 or a cast of 10. You could use puppets for some characters. You could use multimedia. There is plenty of scope for movement, maybe even dance. I envisage music and sound as being integral to the way the story is told. This could be pre-recorded or live. You could even set some of the dialogue to music. Write your own! The possibilities are endless.

This is not only a performance piece. I have written it so that it might be used to stimulate class discussion in a range of subject areas.

You could read the Parliament scene as a lead into a unit of work on Australian politics or history.

You could use the Rainforest scene as part of a discussion about the environment.

Or you might simply like to read a scene in class as a starting point for any discussion.

I wrote *Alice Dreaming* to provoke conversation, debate and thought as well as a vehicle for lots of performers to experience the joy of being on stage. The bottom line is this – whatever you do with *Alice Dreaming,* have some fun.

It's yours to explore and enjoy.

Ned Manning, January 26, 2010.

list of characters

In order of appearance:

Voices	Babies
Alice	Warriors
Cock	Boy
Roach	Old Man
Rat	Housewife
Tom	Shy Girl
Sue	Mother
The Albatross	Daughter
Trees	Dad
Python	Son
Spider	Sister
Wombat	Guards
Sam	Prosecutor
Girls	Judge
Brad	Officials
Boys	Speaker
Miss Victoria	Prime Minister
Rebecca	Leader of Opposition [OPP]
	Politicians

original production notes

The first performance of *Alice Dreaming* was a staged reading at the Australian Theatre for Young people on 12/13 December 2004.

Cast:

Leah Astbury
Harriet Gillies
Patrick Kelly
Karolina Kuligowski
Beejan Olfat
Elle Packam
Gary Panayi
Bella Partridge
Anna Samson
Popi Silk
Skye Staude
Dominic Witkop

Director:

Chris Mead

acknowledgements

The author and publisher wish to thank the following sources for permission to reproduce material:

Images: Keith Saunders, p. ii; Wikimedia Commons/ Public Domain, p. 2; Shutterstock/ Buhantsov Alexey, p. 8/ Rich Lindie, p. 18/ GSK, p. 34/ Vladimir Popovic, p. 44/ Elena Elisseeva, p. 48/ Yuri Arcurs, p. 54/ Children Photos, p. 70/ Gordan, p. 77/ Worldpics, p. 80/ KHZ, p. 92/ Rich Lindie, p. 100/ Neale Cousland, p. 106/ Ilya Genkin, p. 120.

Every effort has been made to trace and acknowledge copyright. The publisher apologises for any accidental infringement and welcomes information that would redress this situation.

scene one

A prison of the mind.

A teenage girl has withdrawn from the world.

She is trapped in her own introspection. It is almost as if she is imprisoned.

She has withdrawn so totally that the outside world hardly exists at all. Her name is ALICE. Everything about her suggests she is hiding.

Family, friends, teachers and even her pets reach out to her but are unable to make contact. Many of those reaching out to ALICE are characters who appear later in the play. They surround ALICE and, in her mind, begin to suffocate her.

This opening scene should be created through movement and music and possibly dance. The following dialogue rains down on ALICE.

VOICES   Come on Alice.

Time to…

Go to bed

Get up

Go out

Do this

Do that

What's the matter?

What's wrong?

What's…

Alice

Alice?

	Alice!!
	Be
	An angel
	A dear
	A friend
	A
	a
	a
ALICE	Be what??
VOICES	Don't
	B
	Like
	That
ALICE	What???
VOICES	Odd
	Even
VOICES	Under
	Over
	Out
	Of
	Bounds
	Boundaries
	Borders
ALICE	Bitch!
VOICES	How
	Dare
	Language
	Own

scene one

	Behaviour
	Your
	Not
	No
	Never
	Ever
	Hear
	Me
	Us
ALICE	No!!!!
	Leave me alone!
	I don't want to go
	Anywhere!!!

She runs.

The CAST chase after her.

She runs in an anti clockwise direction.

It is as if they are chasing her down a drain.

She disappears from sight.

Sound of a bath emptying.

End scene.

scene one

Discussion points

1. Discuss why teenagers often feel isolated. Is it common to feel like the world is literally closing in on you? Ask your classmates what they think.
2. Make a list of the people who are most important to you. Compare and discuss your list with someone else in your class.
3. What is the impact of lots of seemingly disconnected words spoken in rapid fire on a character? Provide an example from the play.
4. Why aren't these words spoken in full sentences? Is the reason for this clear to you?
5. Where do you think that the inspiration for this scene comes from?
6. In pairs, discuss how different meaning is created through movement.

Activities

Theatre is about creating meaning using language, movement and sound. It is a visual medium where the imagination has no bounds. The audience will believe anything as long as you believe it first.

- Make a circle and get one person to stand in the middle.
- The rest of the class slowly circles around them. How does that make them feel? How does the group feel?
- An audience 'reads' our actions on stage much the same as you read a book. So, what do you 'read' when you observe this activity? What does the audience read in this activity?
- If you add some of the words in the text how does this affect the way you 'read' the scene?
- Throughout this activity, be sure to focus on using movement and sound to create meaning.

References

Bend it Like Beckham (2002 film)

Sarah Blasko (Australian singer-songwriter)

Kasey Chambers (Australian country singer-songwriter)

Hannah Montana (American TV series)

My Chemical Romance (American rock band)

Puberty Blues (1981 Australian film)

Taylor Swift (American country singer)

Holly Throsby (Australian singer-songwriter)

The Year My Voice Broke (1987 Australian film)

scene two

A drain.

ALICE is trapped in a drain.

The drain is created by the CAST.

Sound of dripping water. ALICE listens.

ALICE That's…better?

Two COCKROACHES discover her. They are cleaning fastidiously. One of them bumps into her.

COCK Oops.

ROACH What's that?

They inspect ALICE.

COCK Dunno.

ROACH Yuk.

COCK Dirty.

ROACH Filthy.

COCK Under its eyes.

ROACH Needs a good wipe.

COCK Covered in gunk.

COCK tries to wipe some of the eye make-up off ALICE.

ALICE It's not gunk, you idiot.

ROACH Looks like gunk to me.

ALICE It's make-up.

COCK Make-up?

ROACH Disguise?

COCK Fugitive?

ROACH Actor?

COCK   Clown?

They laugh.

ROACH   Very good.

COCK   Thank you.

ROACH   What's that in its hair?

COCK   Bits of rubbish.

ROACH   Edible?

COCK   Everything's edible.

They pull at her hair. ALICE swats them.

COCK   That's

ROACH   Not

COCK   Very

ROACH   Nice.

ALICE   Don't come near me.

COCK   Our job!

ROACH   Our life's work.

COCK   Cock and Roach at your service.

ROACH   The Green Machine.

COCK   Centuries of cleaning.

ROACH   Environmentally sound.

COCK   Five-star rating.

ROACH   Won't know yourself.

COCK   When we've finished.

ROACH   The Pest Wash?

COCK   I should say so.

ALICE   I'm not a pest!

ROACH   Really?

COCK   Not what we hear.

ROACH   Boom boom!

ALICE   Wish I had some Baygon.

They pull back in horror.

COCK   Chemicals!

ROACH   Killer.

COCK   Let's get out of here.

ALICE   Wait.

ROACH   Ruse?

COCK   Trap?

ALICE   Where are you going?

COCK   We're in the survival business sister.

ROACH   We know your type.

They disappear into the darkness.

ALICE   What type?

Silence except for the dripping water.

ALICE pulls something out of her hair and inspects it.

Noises. Scratching. Something is out there. Approaching cautiously.

Eyes flicker in the darkness.

A RAT scampers across the stage. It stops and sniffs.

RAT   Mmm…something smells good.

ALICE   Ohmygod! A rat.

She tries to get away from it but she slips and falls. She is stuck.

ALICE   Smells…

The sound of scratching increases.

ALICE   What's that?

               Helloo?

               Anyone out there?

Chorus of mocking laughter builds. The sound of a cane being rapped on a stone floor. The hubbub dies down.

The RAT peers at ALICE.

RAT Vot 'ave ve 'ere?

ALICE What? What???

A noise, like sharpening teeth.

ALICE What's that noise?

The RAT sniffs her.

ALICE Ugh!

RAT Vot do you vant?

ALICE What do I want?

RAT Vot are you after?

ALICE You're vermin!

RAT Vhy are you here?

ALICE I'm not talking to vermin.

RAT Vhere have you come from?

ALICE None of your business.

RAT Vot have you done?

He nibbles her foot. She kicks at him.

ALICE Don't you dare…

RAT You have spirit.

ALICE Come near me again and I'll kick you to kingdom come!

RAT Vill you now?

ALICE I'm not scared of you.

RAT No? But only move foot. The rest…

He sniffs her.

RAT The rest is…how you say…up for grabbing?

scene two

She tries to wriggle free.

RAT Vho cannot move I think. I know vot it's like. I was caught in a trap once. I escaped. Now zee boot is on zee other foot, no?

ALICE Don't you touch me.

He whispers in her ear.

RAT You've been a naughty little girl, no? Staying out late? Not doing vot you're told?

ALICE Your breath stinks.

RAT Slamming zee door?

ALICE What's it to you?

RAT Do the crime pay the time.

ALICE This is disgusting.

RAT My home! You have ruffled my furs. You have been unkind.

ALICE How can you be unkind to a rat for God's sake?

RAT Zere is no such thing as a free lunch no?

ALICE How can you think of food…

RAT You are very fresh, very sweet, very tasty.

He sniffs her.

ALICE Don't go getting any ideas.

RAT Do you mind if I have a little…taste?

ALICE Rack off!

RAT Just a little nibble. Here and there.

ALICE Get away from me!

RAT Fresh meat. In times like this. Very rare. You are a gift.

ALICE And you're nauseating.

RAT Look at you. Enough meat to feed a small army.

VOICES Leave some for us.

VOICES	Don't take it all for yourself. Be a sport. Just a taste'll do. A wee morsel. A mouthful. A tiny scrap. A little toe perhaps? Keep the wolf from the door. Stave off the rot. Delay the inevitable.
RAT	See? Everyone wants a piece of you. They're starving. They're at the end of their tethers. They beg, they steal, they drink your blood.

The CAST claw their way towards ALICE.

ALICE   Who are they?

RAT   The velcoming committee. Velcome to your nightmare Alice!

ALICE   No, no. Look…

She digs some food out of her pocket.

ALICE   Here.

The RATS stop and sniff.

ALICE   Here ratty ratty.

She has scraps of her dinner in her pockets. She tempts the RATS with them.

ALICE   You like broccoli? Carrots? Beans?

She throws scraps to the hungry RATS. They gobble it up.

ALICE   More?

scene two

She finds more food secreted on her.

ALICE   A sandwich?

She breaks it up and feeds them as if she were feeding chickens.

RAT   Vot about me?

ALICE   For you. Something special.

She takes out a chop.

RAT   Meat? Voo 'ave fresh meat?

The other RATS stop eating and advance on her.

ALICE   Tell them to get away.

The RAT bangs his cane on the ground. They slink back.

ALICE   This is for you.

RAT   For me? How kind.

ALICE   I'll do a deal.

RAT   Deal? I like deal.

ALICE   Let me go and you can have this.

She finds another half-eaten chop.

ALICE   And this.

RAT   A feast!

ALICE   Fit for a king. Can I go now?

RAT   I am a King no? I give, how you say, dispensation.

ALICE   You're a great King, a mighty King, a noble King!

RAT   I am King Rat.

The RAT strides across the stage and ostentatiously pulls a chain.

Sound of a toilet flushing. ALICE is flushed down the drain.

End scene.

scene two

Discussion points

1. Everyone is afraid of something. What are you afraid of?
2. Describe a dream you have had recently. What was it about? Why do you think you had that dream?
3. What is the Underground? What images do you have of the Underground?
4. What meaning does the drain hold?
5. Why does the Rat speak with a funny accent?
6. In pairs, make a list of the environmental issues raised in the scene. Discuss one of these issues in more detail with the class.

Activities

Regardless of who you are, you can play characters of any shape, size or sex. You can play animals or inanimate objects. You can use anything at your disposal to create mood and atmosphere. Lighting helps, but in Shakespeare's day there was no lighting. The situation was the same in Ancient Greece. At both times, theatre relied on the audience's imagination.

- Create a drain by standing very close together or by lying on the ground. Make the drain bend and move. Create sounds using your voices.

- Try to create an underworld that is wet and uncomfortable. What do you have to do differently to make this happen?

- The Ancient Greeks used a *Chorus* both to comment on the action and as a character. The Chorus created mood. The Rats are like a Chorus. They threaten Alice. They move in on her. They make lots of scary sounds. Create the appropriate mood by using sound. Try scratching your fingers on the floor, or tapping and scraping.

- Can you come up with another sound that creates the impression that a drain is a weird place to be?

References

James Bond

The Cold War

World War II concentration camps

Detention centres

Dr Strangelove or: How I Learned to Stop Worrying and Love the Bomb (1964 film)

Oliver Twist (a novel by Charles Dickens)

Refugee camps

Welcome to my Nightmare (1975 album by US singer Alice Cooper)

scene three

The sea.

ALICE has landed in the sea.

The CAST create the waves. They lift her in a gentle, rhythmical motion.

In contrast to the preceding scene it is bright and sunny.

She surfaces.

ALICE   Oh…oh…ohh.

She feels the sun on her face. She has bits of seaweed in her hair.

ALICE   Fresh air! Ahh…the sun…clean water.

She rinses her face.

ALICE   That's better.

The WAVES caress her as she washes herself. It is as if she were in a cleansing, relaxing bath.

For the first time we see her face without make-up.

ALICE   Lovely.

She realises where she is.

ALICE   Hang on…the…I'm in the sea!

She panics.

ALICE   I can't swim. Help! Help!

She waves her arms around frantically. She starts drowning.

ALICE   Help!!!

A couple of DOLPHINS 'swim up' and rescue her. They lift her up.

ALICE   Thank God…

Like hyperactive children, the DOLPHINS are constantly in motion. They nudge her and play with her.

ALICE Hey! That tickles. Don't!! Woops!

She laughs.

ALICE That's fun…ohmygod!

TOM Hello there!

SUE Hi!

TOM Top day!

SUE Ripper isn't it?

ALICE Sharks!

TOM Pardon-moi?

ALICE You're not sharks?

SUE Do we look like sharks?

ALICE I dunno…

TOM You shouldn't always expect the worst Alice.

SUE removes the seaweed from ALICE'S hair.

ALICE How do you know my name?

TOM helps SUE clean any remaining bits and pieces off her.

TOM That's better.

SUE Let's play.

ALICE Play?

TOM Yeah!

SUE Party time.

TOM Mad!

The DOLPHINS toss her around like an inflated beach ball.

SUE You're ok.

scene three

ALICE   Am I?
SUE   Light as a feather.
TOM   Another go?
SUE   Reckon!
ALICE   Hang on…
TOM   Yes?
ALICE   I uh…
SUE   What?
ALICE   I swallowed a mouthful of water.
SUE   Spit it out then!
TOM   Like this.

He demonstrates.

ALICE   It's salty…
SUE   She'll be jake!
TOM   Only water.
ALICE   Make me sick.
SUE   Do you good.
TOM   Clean you up.
SUE   And out.
ALICE   I'd like to get out now.
SUE   Out?
ALICE   My eyes are starting to sting. I'm not a water person.
SUE   Oh?
TOM   Not a water person?
SUE   That's a worry.
TOM   Under the circumstances!
ALICE   Reminds me of swimming lessons.

The DOLPHINS perform a 'routine' during the following.

TOM	Whatcha doin' here then?
SUE	Fall off your yacht?
TOM	Walk the plank?
SUE	Child overboard?
TOM	We get 'em all.
SUE	As busy as feeding time out here at the moment.
TOM	Hardly a day goes by without some odd thing floating by.
SUE	You name it we see it.
TOM	Dragnet fishermen.
SUE	Gas and Oil Drillers.
TOM	Pirates.
SUE	Melting Ice caps.
ALICE	That's quite enough of that!

They keep playing.

SUE	Why?
TOM	What's the matter?
ALICE	Childish?
SUE	Sor-ry!
TOM	Just having fun.
ALICE	I want to get out now.
SUE	You don't want to play with us?
ALICE	No!
SUE	Oh.
TOM	Please.
ALICE	For Pete's sake!

scene three

SUE Who's Pete?
ALICE Stop!!!

Shocked at her aggression they stop.

ALICE So juvenile.
SUE It is?
TOM Better make waves then.

They go to leave.

SUE Keep your eyes peeled.
ALICE Where are you going?
TOM Off to have some fun. What do you reckon?
ALICE You can't just leave me here.
SUE Why not?
TOM Spoilsport!
SUE Plenty of fish in the sea you know.
ALICE You think you're very clever don't you?
SUE Think?
TOM We know we're clever.
ALICE Take me with you!
SUE We would.
TOM If we could.
SUE But we can't.
TOM Sorry.
SUE Not allowed.
TOM They're the rules.
SUE Afraid so.
TOM We used to be able to.
TOM Used to pick up riff raff all the time.

SUE		Not any more.
TOM		Our fins are tied.
SUE		Watch out for sharks.
TOM		You never know what's on the horizon.
SUE		Nice knowin' ya!

They frolic off.

A sudden change in the weather. A storm. Lightning, thunder.

The WAVES are no longer benign but are now menacing. The 'Jaws' theme might introduce a couple of SHARKS as they encircle ALICE.

An ALBATROSS 'flies' in.

The ALBATROSS could be played by one of the CAST, perhaps with wings attached, or it could be a puppet.

The ALBATROSS grabs ALICE. She screams.

ALBATROSS Gotcha!

She screams.

ALBATROSS You're right.

ALICE Help!!!

ALBATROSS Nothing to be frightened of.

ALICE I'm sorry. I'm so sorry. I'll never do it again, whatever it was…

ALBATROSS Calm down.

ALICE I won't answer back. Promise.

She sees that he has wings.

ALICE Ohmygod! Am I dead?

ALBATROSS Not by the look of it.

ALICE Are you an angel?

scene three

ALBATROSS Thank you.

ALICE You're not an angel!

ALBATROSS No.

ALICE You're a bird?

ALBATROSS 'Fraid so.

ALICE Put me down.

ALBATROSS You better come with me.

ALICE Going to feed me to your chicks are you?

ALBATROSS No…

ALICE Eat me yourself?

ALBATROSS Hardly.

ALICE Then let me go!

ALBATROSS Can't do that.

She attacks him.

ALBATROSS Do you mind?

ALICE Stupid bird! You freaked me out.

ALBATROSS Disgruntled passenger…where are the Air Marshalls when you need them?

ALICE Are you deaf?

ALBATROSS A bit.

ALICE All right then.

She bites him.

ALBATROSS Ouch! That hurt.

ALICE I'll bite you again if you don't let me go this minute.

ALBATROSS Can't do that, not in the job description. I'm an Albatross. Our job is to save people. Unless you shoot us down, of course!

ALICE   Silly old fool!

ALBATROSS   See those fins?

ALICE   You can't scare me.

ALBATROSS   You could be a little bit grateful.

ALICE   They're harmless! I was playing with them…

ALBATROSS   White pointers!

ALICE   Ohmygod.

ALBATROSS   Still want me to drop you?

ALICE   I think I'm going to faint…

ALBATROSS   Heard the one about biting the hand that feeds…

ALICE   Or maybe I'm going to have a heart attack.

ALBATROSS   You're not a smoker are you?

ALICE   No but this is pretty trippy!

ALBATROSS   No more biting. Ok?

ALICE   Promise.

She screams.

ALBATROSS   No more screaming either. My hearing's very sensitive. Especially to high-pitched…

ALICE screams again.

ALBATROSS   Teenagers! Climb on my back.

She does.

ALBATROSS   Hold on tight.

ALICE squeezes her eyes tightly shut.

ALBATROSS   Better?

ALICE   No.

ALBATROSS   Trust me.

ALICE	Yeah, right!
ALBATROSS	I'm a bird. I know what I'm doing.
ALICE	I'm scared of heights.
ALBATROSS	You're safe with me.
ALICE	I hate flying!!
ALBATROSS	There's flying and there's flying. This is flying!
ALICE	I'm scared.
ALBATROSS	Go with the flow.
ALICE	What if I fall?

She hangs on for dear life.

ALBATROSS	See down there now? I always think the tops of the waves look like ice cream.
ALICE	I can't open my eyes!
ALBATROSS	If you don't open your eyes you won't see!
ALICE	I can't…
ALBATROSS	Just take a little peek.
ALICE	I don't think I can!
ALBATROSS	No guts no glory!
ALICE	Ohhh…
ALBATROSS	You won't know if you don't try.
ALICE	I…
ALBATROSS	Come on. Be brave. It'll be worth it.
ALICE	I never…I've never been…oh…
ALBATROSS	One. Two. Three. Open Sesame!!

ALICE opens her eyes.

ALICE	Oh my God, oh my God!!

ALBATROSS	See?
ALICE	I haven't got a seat belt.
ALBATROSS	Conquer your fear.
ALICE	We're so far up.
ALBATROSS	What do you think?
ALICE	Freaky.
ALBATROSS	Pretty good eh?
ALICE	My heart! It's beating so fast.
ALBATROSS	Now you know what they mean by a bird's eye view!!!
ALICE	It's gonna burst.
ALBATROSS	Enjoy the ride! Feel the wind in your hair…
ALICE	Were they really sharks?
ALBATROSS	Uh huh.
ALICE	Lucky you spotted them.
ALBATROSS	I like to keep an eye on things.

Pause.

ALICE	This is so weird.
ALBATROSS	Yes?
ALICE	Totally.
ALBATROSS	I know.
ALICE	Where are we going?
ALBATROSS	I'm heading south.
ALICE	I'll come with you.
ALBATROSS	That might be a bit tricky.
ALICE	Why?
ALBATROSS	I'm heading south to…you know…

scene three

ALICE No…

ALBATROSS Well, it's a bit delicate.

ALICE Why?

ALBATROSS You're a young girl, I'm an old bird…

ALICE So?

ALBATROSS It's biological.

ALICE What is?

ALBATROSS The reason I'm heading south. It's the only time I go to Land.

ALICE I don't get it…

ALBATROSS I'm a bird. I migrate. I fly south to you know…

ALICE …breed! The breeding season! Oh, I get it! You're going to 'chase a bit of tail', as my Dad says.

ALBATROSS Please! I'm an old fashioned kind of bird. That kind of talk…

ALICE Where are we now?

ALBATROSS That's the Arafura Sea.

ALICE Oh. What's that?

ALBATROSS Don't you do Geography?

ALICE Who does Geography?

ALBATROSS You should.

ALICE What would you know?

ALBATROSS Good point.

She points.

ALICE Is that land?

ALBATROSS Yep.

ALICE I want to get off.

ALBATROSS You sure?
ALICE If I can't go with you.
ALBATROSS I don't think Antarctica would be your speed.
ALICE What would you know?
ALBATROSS I could take you somewhere more…hospitable.
ALICE Down there.
ALBATROSS Pretty isolated.
ALICE Good.
ALABTROSS Not many…people.
ALICE Excellent.
ALBATROSS You don't like people?
ALICE I don't like sticky beaks.

The ALBATROSS inspects his beak.

ALICE I'm going to shut my eyes now.

The ALBATROSS heads towards land.

ALBATROSS You up for a challenge?
ALICE What's with all the questions?
ALBATROSS Sorry.
ALICE You're like all the rest of them.
ALBATROSS Who?
ALICE Them.
ALBATROSS Just shooting the breeze.
ALICE I'm sick of it.
ALBATROSS My bad.
ALICE Tell me when we're there ok?
ALBATROSS You're the boss.

scene three

The ALBATROSS 'banks' towards the mainland.

ALBATROSS Hold on tight!

They head towards Land.

End scene.

scene three

Discussion points

1. Name the oceans that surround Australia.
2. What were the early explorers looking for when they came into this region?
3. What do you know about dolphins? Why do you think many people consider them special creatures?
4. How has pollution affected the oceans? Can you find examples of oil spills that have affected the environment? When was the latest one?
5. What is the greatest threat to the Great Barrier Reef?
6. In small groups, discuss the phrase 'Global Warming'.
7. What do we mean by the term 'over-fishing'?
8. Is our fear of sharks reasonable? How should we treat sharks?
9. How long have so-called 'boat people' been coming to Australia?
10. What do you know about the 'Children Overboard' incident?

Activities

All the creative arts are connected. In the theatre we bring them all together to create magic. Visual imagery is a fundamental part of theatre. Costume and set design create worlds in which the audience is transported from the ordinariness of their own lives.

- Try to create a sense of the sea through movement. Use whole bodies to create the rhythms of the sea. Start with calm and then imagine the wind blowing up a storm. Add sound to enhance this.
- Explore the use of lighting to enhance the threatening nature of the storm. If you have access to theatre lights, experiment with how you might use them to create the effect of lightning. You might be able to achieve the same effect using torches in a darkened space.

scene three

- Now use a different form of lighting to indicate that the sun has burst through. Again, if you don't have theatre lighting, you might go from darkness to torch flashes to lights on!
- How might you create dolphins? Try doing this as a kind of dance. The dolphins are like playful kids who can't sit still.
- Contrast this with the kind of movements a shark might make. Add the theme music from the film *Jaws*. (Everyone will get it then!)
- Play with costume ideas to create dolphins and sharks. The dolphins might wear party clothes while the sharks wear dark glasses.
- Read the poem 'The Rime of the Ancient Mariner' by Samuel Taylor Coleridge.
- Think about how you are going to create the Albatross. If you are really adventurous you might like to make a big puppet. Or you could make some papier mâche wings. Or you might have the Albatross costumed as a wise old bird like Gandalf from Tolkien's *The Lord of the Rings*. The possibilities are endless and you don't have to be literal. Remember this is the theatre. Anything is possible.

References

'Botany Bay – Farewell to Old England Forever'

Dark Victory (David Marr and Marian Wilkinson)

The Discovery of Australia (Captain James Cook)

Obsession and Discovery (Captain James Cook)

'The Rime of the Ancient Mariner' (Samuel Taylor Coleridge)

scene four

A rainforest.

The CAST create a tropical rainforest. Although dark and imposing it is alive with life, much of which is invisible to the naked eye. The sounds are particularly distinctive and, to an outsider, quite disturbing. The light has an eerie quality as it shines through a gap in the canopy.

ALICE 'lands' in this alien environment. She has never seen anything like it.

ALICE   Middle Earth? Has he dropped me in Middle Earth?

The TREES move.

TREES   Middle Earth!

ALICE   Wha…

The TREES groan.

ALICE   What was that?

TREES   Gondwanaland.

ALICE   Someone there?

TREES   You are standing in Gondwanaland.

She checks out the TREES.

ALICE   Big trees. Must be pretty old.

TREES   Old? We're not old. We're ancient.

She gasps.

TREES   We are survivors on the oldest living continent.

She is shocked.

TREES   What is your agenda?

ALICE   I…I don't have an… agenda.

TREES	You are human?
ALICE	Yeees…
TREES	You have an agenda.

The TREES move. Creaking, shaking leaves. A screech in the canopy.

ALICE	Ohmygod! What was that?
TREES	We need to stretch.

A cacophony of sound in the stillness as the TREES movement scatters the fauna. ALICE covers her ears.

ALICE	The noise!
TREES	Fear is everywhere.
ALICE	Fear? I'm not scared! You can't scare me.

A ROCK PYTHON slithers up to her.

PYTHON	Sssomething's suspiciousss…she's doesn't smell like swine!

ALICE screams.

PYTHON	Ssoo…swindler is she?
ALICE	Snake!
PYTHON	Sure am sweetie!
ALICE	Sugar!
PYTHON	Sumptuous swine swell snakies stomach.
ALICE	Swine? Pigs?
PYTHON	S'true. Seen something similar?

ALICE is so scared she stutters.

ALICE	Ssss…something for you to sss…swallow?
PYTHON	Struth! She's sharp.
ALICE	I…ah…sss…swine…certainly! Sss…spied some somewhere. See?

scene four

She points.

PYTHON Super!

ALICE So long snakey.

PYTHON Superb. See ya.

The PYTHON slithers off. ALICE clenches her fist in triumph.

ALICE Sorted! Sensational sibilance.

A MOSQUITO buzzes her.

ALICE Ah ha!

She swats it.

ALICE Take that!

A SPIDER scurries into view.

SPIDER Hey! Whattya doing?

ALICE tries to stomp on it but it eludes her.

ALICE I hate spiders.

SPIDER Why?

ALICE Because I do.

SPIDER Oh great!

ALICE Only good spider is dead one.

She chases the SPIDER.

SPIDER Hey stop it willya? What's the problem? Too hairy for you? Too many legs? Listen sister willya stop tryin' to kill me? I done nothin' to you. You're the one who owes me. You just killed me entrée.

ALICE taunts the SPIDER with the dead MOSQUITO.

ALICE Come and get it you ugly-looking…

SPIDER Hate to tell you babe but you ain't no oil painting yourself.

ALICE	Rack off hairy legs.
SPIDER	All right then. Arm wrestle you for it. Which arm?
ALICE	I don't want your bloody mosquito.
SPIDER	Language!
ALICE	Take it.
SPIDER	You sure?
ALICE	What am I going to do with a dead mozzie?
SPIDER	A rare species!
ALICE	Is it deadly?
SPIDER	You. A considerate human. Can I find you on the web?
ALICE	Just take it. It's yours.
SPIDER	You're all right. Catch ya.

The SPIDER drags the MOSQUITO off. ALICE looks around. Apart from bush sounds all is quiet.

ALICE	Cool.

She sits on a 'rock' and huddles into a ball.

ALICE	At last.

She takes out her iPod.

ALICE	Silence.

She rocks back and forth. As if on cue the 'roc" starts moving too.

ALICE	Ooo…oh….ohhhh! The earth's movin' for me. Feels… oh….quite nice actually…

The 'rock' tips her off. It is a WOMBAT.

WOMBAT	Get off me!
ALICE	Hey!
WOMBAT	Who gave you permission to sit…

ALICE	For God's sake! A talking rock!!
WOMBAT	I beg your pardon?
ALICE	Is there no end…
WOMBAT	I've been called a lot of things in my life but never a rock!
ALICE	I'm not going to talk to a rock.
WOMBAT	I thought 'muddled headed' was bad enough but 'rock'!! I've got my pride you know.
ALICE	A wombat? I didn't realise…
WOMBAT	No. No one does.
ALICE	How was I to know…
WOMBAT	Minding my own business. Enjoying a quiet nap. Trying to avoid extinction. Like all of us. Come to clear fell have you?
ALICE	What are you on about?

The TREES rumble.

WOMBAT	Turn all this into woodchips too eh? That your scheme? Not satisfied with chopping down the rest of the country you've got to come up here too have you?
ALICE	Wasn't my idea.
WOMBAT	Can't you just leave us alone? anymore thanks to you. Or is that your Concrete the lot! That'd be right.
ALICE	You want to be alone?
WOMBAT	Are you a diversionary tactic?
ALICE	What are you rabbiting on about?
WOMBAT	While I'm talking to you, your mates are sharpening their chain saws. Is that the story?
ALICE	Mates? What mates? I haven't got any mates.
WOMBAT	So? That's your plan?

ALICE   Will you shut up?

WOMBAT   I don't trust you.

ALICE   Do I look like I care?

WOMBAT   Can't blame me. With your track record.

ALICE   I'm all sticky.

WOMBAT   Oh yes it's all heating up all right. Thanks to you lot.

ALICE sees a BILLABONG.

ALICE   I'm gonna cool off in that lake.

WOMBAT   That's not a lake.

ALICE   Whatever.

WOMBAT   That's a billabong.

ALICE goes to move.

ALICE   Great.

WOMBAT   Jump in there you'll get a nasty surprise.

ALICE   When I want your advice I'll ask for it.

The WOMBAT stops her.

WOMBAT   See that?

ALICE   That log?

WOMBAT   That 'log' will have you for breakfast if you go anywhere near it. It's a crocodile. They love tourists. Their staple diet these days.

ALICE   I'm not a tourist!

WOMBAT   What are you looking for then?

ALICE   I'm not looking for company that's for sure?

WOMBAT   What do you want?

ALICE   How would I know?

WOMBAT   There's a road through there.

ALICE	Where's it lead to?
WOMBAT	Wherever you want it to go.
ALICE	Nowhere?
WOMBAT	If that's where you want to go.
ALICE	What's out there?
WOMBAT	Not much.
ALICE	Good.
WOMBAT	Whatever you do, don't go wandering off the beaten track. Stay on the straight and narrow.
ALICE	Why does everyone feel the need to give me advice?

She leaves the WOMBAT.

WOMBAT	Watch out for the road trains. And strange men in four-wheel drives!

End scene.

scene four

Discussion points

1. What is a rainforest? Why are trees so important to the life cycle?
2. What is Gondwanaland? Where did the word come from?
3. Goannas, crocodiles and lots of other native species camouflage themselves. Why do they do this?
4. Create a list of endangered species in Australia. How are imported animals threatening native animals?
5. What do you think is different about our attitude to the land and the attitude held by Indigenous Australians?
6. Why do we have National Parks?
7. How old is Australia?
8. What is the difference between a billabong and a lake?

Activities

When actors move from one scene to another they are making a transition. One of the joys of theatre is watching transitions. These are part of the magic as a scene is transformed from one place to another. We can bring props in and take them out. We don't need to do this in darkness. Audiences love to be part of the magic of theatre making.

- Research the ecology of the rainforest. Focus on the complex relationship between plants and animals.
- Make a map of Australia before European colonisation. How much of Australia was covered by rainforest before colonisation?
- Have a debate arguing the case for and against logging in wilderness areas.
- Make a list of all the National Parks in Australia.
- Create a soundscape that represents the sounds of the Australian landscape.

- Investigate how you might create the different sounds in this scene, including silence.
- In groups, create a rainforest. Remember how entangled it is in its natural state. You might do this as a movement exercise.
- Study a native animal and its habitat, and re-create it's movements in class. Do the same with an imported animal.
- Improvise a scene where a native animal is threatened by an imported one. Focus on tiny details.

References

Australian Wilderness Photo Gallery (http://ginini.com/wilderness/galleries.html)

'Beds are Burning' (song by Australian band Midnight Oil)

'If a Tree Falls' (song by Bruce Cockburn)

Steve Irwin and Australia Zoo

Kakadu National Park

The Lord of the Rings (trilogy of books by J.R.R.Tolkien)

The Wilderness Society (http://www.wilderness.org.au/)

scene five

The road.

The landscape has transformed. The rainforest has given way to a seemingly endless stretch of empty desert. In contrast to the rainforest there is no sign of life out here.

The HOT SUN beats down on ALICE. It could be created by the CAST.

At first she walks along happily alone, listening to music on her iPod.

It is ALICE'S Yellow Brick Road. She waves to passing traffic. A TRUCK slows down. She waves it on. This is what she was searching for. Solitude.

As she walks on the HOT SUN becomes increasingly oppressive. She begins to realise that she doesn't have any water.

ALICE   Water? I haven't got any water.

Sound of another TRUCK.

ALICE   Hey!

She tries to stop it but it accelerates past her. Another TRUCK does the same thing. ALICE becomes increasingly desperate. There is a sense of convoys of TRUCKS whizzing past her in both directions while she is caught in the middle. She begins to panic.

She stumbles off the highway and out into the desert.

She starts hallucinating. She 'sees' ICE CREAM VENDORS, DRINK MACHINES, GELATO BARS and maybe the entrance to a SWIMMING POOL.

She rushes towards these mirages but they exist only in her imagination.

She becomes increasingly desperate, spiraling out of control until finally collapsing.

End scene.

scene five

Discussion points

1. What is the difference between the ecologies of the rainforest and the desert?
2. Why is inland Australia so inhospitable?
3. What happened to the explorers Burke and Wills?
4. Do Australians have a special relationship with the sun? Discuss in small groups.
5. What films or books might have inspired this scene?
6. Why is our natural environment often so threatening?
7. Create a list of films, poems, novels, plays and artworks that have been inspired by our relationship with the natural environment.
8. How do we create fantasy and dreams on stage?

Activities

Offstage sound creates mood and introduces characters. Sound takes us into new places. Sound can tell us whether we're near the sea. It can tell us that a big truck is roaring past. It can be threatening and even frightening.

- Try to create the transition from the rainforest to the desert. Do this as a group. Focus on the contrast between the two environments and investigate how you might show this.
- Using movement, create the sun. Make it threatening. You might do this by circling and bearing down on someone.
- Draw images of the desert on butcher's paper. Use them to create a desert landscape. Keep props to a minimum. Remember you have to bring them on stage during the transition.
- Create the dreamscape Alice sees when she is hallucinating. This might be projected onto a screen or a wall.

scene five

- Play with creating the sound of a big road truck zooming past.
- Use filmic images to create Alice's hallucination.

References

Blue Sky Mining (1990 album by Australian band Midnight Oil)

Albert Namatjira (Indigenous Australian artist)

Sidney Nolan (Australian artist)

Samson and Delilah (2009 Australian film)

Sunday Too Far Away (1975 Australian film)

Wake in Fright (1971 Australian film)

Brett Whiteley (Australian artist)

Fred Williams (Australian artist)

The Wizard of Oz (book by L. Frank Baum; 1939 film)

Wolf Creek (2005 Australian film)

scene six

A desert.

ALICE lies in a heap, exposed to the elements and seemingly without hope.

A spurt of water lands on her face. She looks up as the ALBATROSS appears.

ALBATROSS Thirsty?

At first she thinks it is another mirage. The ALBATROSS gives her another spurt.

ALBATROSS You look like you need a drink.

ALICE I'm dying of thirst.

ALBATROSS Here.

He gives her a drink.

ALICE Thank you.

ALBATROSS You need to rehydrate.

She drinks.

ALICE You must think I'm an idiot.

ALBATROSS I didn't say a word.

ALICE I was so scared.

ALBATROSS Don't blame you.

ALICE You are an angel!

ALBATROSS Someone's got to keep an eye on you.

ALICE My guardian angel.

She gives the ALBATROSS a hug.

ALICE I thought you didn't fly inland?

ALBATROSS	I don't, if I can avoid it!
ALICE	How can anything survive out here?
ALBATROSS	I'm probably not the best person to ask that question. More water?

She drinks.

ALICE	Thanks.
ALBATROSS	Let's get going then.
ALICE	This is so annoying.
ALBATROSS	All aboard!
ALICE	I know what you're thinking.
ALBATROSS	I'm thinking I want to get out of here before I expire.
ALICE	Sorry.
ALBATROSS	What was that?
ALICE	I said sorry.
ALBATROSS	I thought's that's what you said! On you get.

She climbs aboard.

ALBATROSS	Let's put this behind us.
ALICE	Lets.

She leans forward and hugs him as they take off.

ALBATROSS	Where to?
ALICE	No idea.
ALBATROSS	We'll head for the coast first.
ALICE	Sounds good to me.
ALBATROSS	Ok?
ALICE	Yep. I am now.
ALBATROSS	No girl is an island, Alice.

ALICE looks down.

ALICE Any ideas?

ALBATROSS Maybe.

ALICE I'm in your hands.

ALBATROSS Wings.

ALICE It's pretty cool up here. When you get used to it.

ALBATROSS Even birds have to learn how to fly.

ALICE lets go. She sits up and extends her arms.

ALBATROSS Better?

ALICE Way.

They fly.

ALBATROSS Ok?

ALICE Oh yeah.

ALBATROSS Good-oh.

ALICE Yo!

ALBATROSS Not bad eh?

ALICE This is the maddest fun ever.

ALBATROSS Up for some real flying?

ALICE Sure am dude.

ALABTROSS Dude?

ALICE Go for it!

The ALBATROSS gives her a 'joy ride'.

ALICE screams with delight. They fly through some clouds.

ALBATROSS How was that?

ALICE Awesome!!

ALBATROSS Happy customer eh?

ALICE Very happy.

ALBATROSS That's what we like.

ALICE You're the best.

ALABTROSS Enjoy the flight.

ALICE Aye aye captain!

They pass over the desert and head towards the coast.

End scene.

scene six

Discussion points

1. What do you think the Albatross is doing for Alice?
2. Halfway through the play, how has her attitude to the Albatross changed?
3. In small groups see how many stories you can think of in which an older character guides a younger character.
4. What is meant by the term 'guardian angel'?

Activities

Plays are inspired by all sorts of things. Often films, paintings and even songs provide the inspiration for a scene. Playwrights often have a visual image in their head when they write a scene.

- Create an image of Alice 'flying'. You might like to look at the poster for the film *Titanic* (1997) as inspiration.
- Draw or use Photoshop to create a poster for *Alice Dreaming* using this scene as inspiration.
- Think about how you might show Alice flying. Using multimedia? By having her elevated? Remember in theatre you don't need to be literal. An audience will accept a character is 'flying' if they tell us they are. That is the magic of theatre. An audience will 'suspend its disbelief' to believe whatever we ask them to as long as we are committed to it.

References

Harry Potter series (J.K. Rowling)

The Lord of the Rings (J.R.R. Tolkien)

'Meditation XVII: No Man is an Island' (a 1624 poem by John Donne)

Titanic (1997 film)

scene seven

A beach.

A beach. It could be Surfers Paradise.

A group of TEENAGE GIRLS lie in the sun. They are identical: their hair, their make-up, their swimmers. They are perfectly in sync with each other. They all turn over and apply tanning lotion. This is a well-rehearsed routine.

First the legs, then the arms, then the faces. This is a very cool scene.

They look up as a shadow passes over them. They register their disgust.

ALICE 'lands'. In contrast to the GIRLS, she looks a mess. Her clothes are disheveled and she is exhausted.

She walks towards the GIRLS. They feign indifference. ALICE waves meekly to them. They turn as one to reject her. After a moment ALICE decides to sit nearby. All eyes turn to watch her as she passes them. Even though she becomes immediately invisible to them, she edges herself closer and closer towards where they are sitting.

SAM	Did you hear about Annabelle?
ALL	No?

They all raise themselves on one arm and listen to SAM.

SAM	Well…
ALL	Go on…
SAM	Should I?
ALL	Yes!
SAM	It's pretty bad.
ALL	Please.

SAM	You sure?
ALL	Tell us!
SAM	I don't know if I should…
ALL	What is it?
SAM	You won't believe this…
ALL	What?
SAM	Ok.
ALL	What's she done now?
SAM	She got a tongue ring!
ALL	A tongue ring?
SAM	A tongue ring!
ALL	Try-hard!
SAM	Exactly.
ALL	She's a bitch.
SAM	She sure is.
ALL	So up herself.
SAM	Did you hear what she said?
ALL	No?
SAM	About us?
ALL	No?
SAM	She said…
ALL	Yes?
SAM	She said…
ALL	Yes??
SAM	She said we were bitches!
ALL	The bitch!
SAM	I so hate her.

scene seven

ALL So do I.

SAM I'm so glad we kicked her out of our group.

ALL Me too.

SAM Bitch!

ALL Bitch!

A GIRL approaches.

ALL Hi Annabelle!

ANNABELLE Hi!

SAM Wanna sit with us?

ANNABELLE Oh…

ALL Go on!

SAM There's plenty of room.

ANNABELLE Maybe…

SAM You wanna…

ANNABELLE What?

SAM You wanna…

ANNABELLE Yeah?

SAM Show us your tongue ring.

ALL Please?

They crowd around her.

SAM Please.

She does.

ALL Cool!!

SAM That's so cool.

ALL You wanna come back to our group?

ANNABELLE Those other girls are bitches.

ALL	No?
ANNABELLE	You know what they said?
ALL	No?
ANNABELLE	They said I was a bitch.
ALL	No!!
SAM	Sit with us. They're such…

A group of BOYS approach from different angles. Like a posse. They too are identical. Identical boardies, identical sunnies, identical posture. They exchange handshakes, a ritual, with an air of affected casualness.

BOYS	Yo?
BRAD	Hey dudes.
BOYS	What's doin'?
BRAD	New sunnies.
BOYS	Cool man!
BRAD	Way to go.
BOYS	Way to go.
SLOW BOY *[catching up]*	Way to go.
GIRLS	Hi guys.

The BOYS take up macho poses. They look like statues of Greek gods.

BRAD	Surf's stuffed.
BOYS	Yeah man.
BRAD	Life's shit.
BOYS	Yeah.
BRAD	Let's get wasted.
BOYS	Yeah!
BRAD	Let's get trashed.
BOYS	Yeah.

scene seven

BRAD Let's...
BOYS Yeah.
SAM You guys are so cool.
GIRLS Yeah.
BRAD Hot babes!
BOYS Yeah.
BRAD Reckon we'll talk to them?
BOYS Yeah!
BRAD Not by myself.
BOYS Nah.
BRAD Back me up?
BOYS Yeah man.
BRAD Hi Sam.
SAM Hi Brad.
BRAD Watcha doin'?
SAM Hangin' round, you know.
BOYS Yeah.
GIRLS Yeah.
BOYS Cool.
GIRLS Cool.
SAM You guys seen Annabelle's tongue ring?
BRAD You kidding?
GIRLS It's so cool.
BOYS Let's see.

They crowd around ANNABELLE who displays her tongue ring.

ALICE is now close enough to look. She joins the crowd around ANNABELLE.

ALICE	Ahh…excuse me?

They turn as one and stare at her.

SAM	Excuse me!
GIRLS	Who are you?
ALICE	Oh…hi…
SAM	What do you want?

The GIRLS pose for ALICE. A look of practiced contempt.

ALICE	I just…
SAM	Yeah?
GIRLS	Where's she get off?
ALICE	…kinda flew in.
GIRLS	Dressing like that.
SAM	Talking like that.
GIRLS	Looking like that.
ALICE	I had a bit of a…long story…
GIRLS	Check out her hair.
SAM	Can you believe it?
ALICE	I'm sorry…I'm a bit of a mess…

The BOYS notice ALICE.

BRAD	Guys! Hot or not?
BOYS	Hot.
BRAD	Hot!
SAM	Looking at something?
ALICE	Oh…me?
SAM	Nah, your shadow…
BOYS	Talk to her Brad.

scene seven

BRAD   Back me up.

GIRLS   This is our place.

The GIRLS turn their backs on her. The BOYS push BRAD forward.

BRAD   Ahh…hi!

ALICE   Oh, hello.

BRAD grunts.

ALICE   Great beach.

He grunts again.

ALICE   I've never been here before.

Another grunt.

ALICE   Bit of an inner-city girl.

BOYS   Talk to her Brad.

BRAD   What'll I say?

BOYS   We dunno.

ALICE   The water's so blue!

BRAD   Um…

ALICE   And you're all so brown!

BRAD   Yeah…

ALICE   I mean, look at me!

BRAD   Nah…

ALICE   And the sun!!

BRAD   Right…

ALICE   So hot.

BRAD   Hot!

BOYS   Nail her Brad!

BRAD	Totally.
GIRLS	Sam?
SAM	Pretend not to care.

Affected disinterest from the GIRLS. BRAD builds confidence and the BOYS crowd around ALICE.

BRAD	Ahhh…hey babe!
ALICE	Yes?
BRAD	How's it goin'?
ALICE	Oh…it's…pretty good, I think.
BOYS	Way to go Brad!
ALICE	Pretty good.
BRAD	Wild.
ALICE	Wild? Yeah, wild!
BRAD	Awesome.
ALICE	Excellent!
BRAD	Out there!
ALICE	Brilliant!
BRAD	Mad!
ALICE	Wicked!
BRAD	Insane in the membrane!
ALICE	Ahhh…
BRAD	Way to go!
BRAD	That's so cool…isn't it guys?
BOYS	Out there man!
BRAD	I'm Brad.
BOYS	We're the boys!
SAM	Ohmygod!

scene seven

GIRLS	Do something!
SAM	What'll I…

She suddenly pushes into the circle followed by the GIRLS.

SAM	Hi!!
ALICE	Hello…
GIRLS	Hi!!!
SAM	Maddest look.
GIRLS	So cool.
BRAD	Unreal…
BOYS	Yeah!
SAM	We're so uncool.
GIRLS	Where'd you get…
ALICE	Pardon?
SAM	Your…you know…that…
GIRLS	Your crazy outfit!
SAM	Yeah, like…
GIRLS	Your hair!
SAM	And everything…
GIRLS	It's all so cool.
SAM	How do you…
ALICE	How come I look like this?
SAM	Tell us?
GIRLS	Please.
ALICE	You don't want to know.

Before she can explain the GIRLS tear at whatever they are wearing, ruffle their hair and smudge their make-up to achieve ALICE'S dishevelled look.

ALICE	This is so good.
ALL	Check it!
ALICE	I'm going to lie in the sun and get a really good tan.
ALL	Fully sick bro!

They all lie in 'tanning' poses. ALICE watches them and then imitates.

BRAD	Want some oil?
ALICE	Yes please.

She applies oil.

SAM	Stay away from Factor 30+. It stops you getting brown.
ALICE	Ohh that sun!

The CAST circle her and, like the SUN, smile benignly on ALICE.

BRAD	Hey guys!
BOYS	Brad?
BRAD	The time?

The SUN gradually becomes more and more oppressive.

BOYS	We've got footy training…
GIRLS	We've got netball.
BRAD	We betta split.
SAM	See ya Alice!
GIRLS	She's so cool
BOYS	She's so hot.

They exit.

The SUN begins to 'cook' ALICE.

ALICE is left alone. She practices sitting like the GIRLS, flicking her hair, arching her back and so on.

scene seven

She sizzles and is about to be engulfed by what has become a fiery furnace when the ALBATROSS creates a shadow.

ALICE   Hey!!

ALBATROSS   What did I say about the sun?

He shades her with his wings.

ALICE   I'm trying to get a tan!

ALBATROSS   You're burning up.

ALICE   Will you get out of the way?

ALBATROSS   I didn't risk my life and fly all the way into the Simpson Desert so you could cook yourself like some irresponsible…

ALICE   Teenager?

ALBATROSS   Potato chip!

ALICE   I want to get brown.

ALBATROSS   I want to be an eagle!

ALICE   I'm as white as a ghost.

ALBATROSS   I'm as old as Methuselah!

ALICE   I need some colour.

ALBATROSS   I need a drink!

ALICE   I need a friend.

ALBATROSS   If you think I've got nothing better to do than fly around the place rescuing you then you've got another thing coming.

He stops his lecture.

ALBATROSS   What did you say?

ALICE   You heard.

ALBATROSS   Ohhh…

ALICE	Don't 'ohhh' me. Help me.
ALBATROSS	Mmm.
ALICE	'Mmm…' What does that mean?
ALBATROSS	It means I'm thinking.
ALICE	And?
ALBATROSS	I'm not sure I can.
ALICE	I'm never gonna be like them. I don't wanna be like them. But…but I wouldn't mind one friend. Apart from you that is.
ALBATROSS	That's nice.
ALICE	Well?
ALBATROSS	I wouldn't know where to start.
ALICE	Can you take me somewhere else?
ALBATROSS	I could but …
ALICE	What?
ALBATROSS	Why don't you dig a bit deeper.
ALICE	Get my head out of the sand?
ALBATROSS	Something like that.
ALICE	How long have I got?
ALBATROSS	The rest of your life?
ALICE	That all?

The ALBATROSS looks out to sea.

ALBATROSS	Fishermen heading out.
ALICE	You're going?
ALBATROSS	Nature calls.
ALICE	Please!
ALBATROSS	Gotta take your chances. I always follow the fishing leet! Pick up a free feed. See ya.

He takes off.

His wings flapping cause some bits of paper to fly about.

ALICE   Careful! You're making a mess.

She rushes around picking them up. One catches her eye.

ALICE   Job vacancies.

End scene.

scene seven

Discussion points

1. As a class, discuss the nature of peer pressure. Why do you think people feel obliged to follow the leader or engage in risky behaviour?

2. How difficult is it to follow your own instincts? In small groups, discuss a time when you followed your own instincts as opposed to the 'mob'.

3. What role do you think the media play in shaping how teenagers see themselves and others?

4. In small groups, discuss the following: What is body image? How has the perception of what is beautiful changed throughout time? Why are we preoccupied with body image? What affect has this preoccupation had on teenage life?

5. Define celebrity. Make a list of celebrities. What are they famous for? Do you think they are good role models?

6. Why do you think that people lie in the sun trying to get a tan when the evidence suggests that this could lead to skin cancer?

Activities

Choreographed movement creates meaning as well as establishing mood and atmosphere. A group of performers moving in unison tells the audience something. This is the language of the theatre as much as words are.

- Collect some images associated with 'grunge'. Research where this look came from.

- Create a collage of things you associate with Australian beach culture.

- Play a game of 'follow the leader'. What happens when someone changes direction to go their own way?

- Using the dialogue at the top of the scene, choreograph actions to match the words. You might want to begin with some music and movement before you start the dialogue. If you're really adventurous, try this as a dance sequence like in a musical.

- Now reverse the roles (a role swap). Have girls play the boys and vice versa. What discoveries did you make?
- Collect images from all forms of media that influence our attitude to body shape. Contrast these with some historical images of 'beauty'. (You could download some from the web.)
- Create a fashion parade using your school uniform. See how many variations of wearing the uniform you can come up with!
- Design costumes appropriate for this scene. You might want to draw them or use Photoshop. Imagine you are a costume designer and present the images as a design portfolio.
- Find music that might underscore this scene.

References

Ancient Greek sculpture

Marilyn Monroe (20th century US actress)

Peter Paul Rubens (17th century Flemish Baroque painter)

'The Secrets of Grunge Design' (2008 article in *Smashing Magazine*)

Surfer Girl (1963 album by US band The Beach Boys)

Surf magazines

Teen magazines

scene eight

A child care centre.

A cacophony of BABIES crying.

REBECCA, a girl ALICE'S age, rushes around changing nappies and trying to settle the BABIES. She is like a slave to MISS VICTORIA. She wears a name tag.

ALICE knocks on the door.

VICTORIA   Get that!

REBECCA obeys and returns to work. ALICE walks into the mayhem.

VICTORIA   What do you want?
ALICE   I…I read about the job.
VICTORIA   Did you now?
ALICE   Yeess…I'm sorry maybe I should come back…

She freezes.

VICTORIA   Well?
ALICE   Uh?
VICTORIA   I haven't got all day.
ALICE   I…uh…sorry it's just that…
VICTORIA   Yes?
ALICE   You look like my Drama teacher.
VICTORIA   Do I? Well isn't that fascinating? As you can see we're rather up to our necks in it, so either come in and get to work or on your bike.

REBECCA wrestles with a particularly difficult BABY.

VICTORIA   Well? Come on. We haven't got all day.

ALICE I…ah…what does the Albatross say, 'no guts no glory'?

VICTORIA Is that a yes?

ALICE Yes, yes!

VICTORIA hands her a change bag.

VICTORIA Change that.

ALICE Ah…

VICTORIA You'll soon learn.

She marches off. She takes up a position where she can keep an eye on proceedings. She talks on her phone, works on her laptop but watches REBECCA and ALICE like a hawk.

ALICE stares. The BABY looks at ALICE. ALICE looks at the BABY. The BABY screams. REBECCA comes to her rescue.

REBECCA Here. I'll show you.

She changes the nappy. ALICE nearly faints.

ALICE Thanks.

A BABY screams. REBECCA puts a dummy back in her mouth. The dummy looks like a VB stubby. The BABY sucks enthusiastically.

ALICE That's not…

REBECCA gestures towards VICTORIA.

REBECCA Don't ask.

She rushes to another BABY.

ALICE Can I help?

REBECCA Be great.

ALICE I think this one's…

scene eight

REBECCA is flat out settling the BABY she's with. ALICE grabs the nappy bag.

ALICE   Here goes.

REBECCA   Good luck.

During the following exchange ALICE struggles with a nappy whilst REBECCA does her best to settle the rest.

ALICE   This isn't as easy at it looks.

REBECCA   Sssh.

ALICE   Is she spying on us?

She indicates towards VICTORIA who is watching.

REBECCA   Don't let her see us talking.

ALICE   Why not?

REBECCA makes a 'slitting throat' gesture.

REBECCA   Against the rules.

ALICE   Some rules are made to be broken.

A siren rings out. Lights drop. The BABIES stop crying and immediately fall asleep. REBECCA whispers.

REBECCA   Sleep time.

REBECCA grabs a bucket and a cloth and starts scrubbing the floor. ALICE helps her.

ALICE   Take a break. You look like…

REBECCA   Crap?

ALICE   No, no. I didn't mean…

REBECCA   It's ok.

ALICE   I mean tired. Worn out. You do this all on your own?

REBECCA   Mostly. No one ever stays.

ALICE   I can see why.

REBECCA   Yeah.

ALICE   But you do?

REBECCA   No choice.

VICTORIA is watching. ALICE whispers.

ALICE   She can't hear us now can she?

REBECCA   I can't afford to lose this job.

VICTORIA marches towards them.

VICTORIA   You wouldn't be talking would you young lady?

REBECCA   No Miss Victoria.

VICTORIA   You know the consequences?

REBECCA   Yes Miss Victoria.

VICTORIA   Now. Here is the timetable.

She hands the timetable to ALICE.

VICTORIA   Learn this off by heart.

ALICE   What is it?

VICTORIA   Everything you need to know.

ALICE reads.

ALICE   0900 Feed. Yoghurt. Non-fat.

             0930 Play. Ball skills. Non-competitive.

             1000 Read. Language for the Gifted Toddler…

             Gifted Toddler?

VICTORIA   This Centre caters for the Advanced Baby. We have a Gifted and Talented stream.

scene eight

ALICE Wow.

1020 Free Time.

That was 'Free Time'?

VICTORIA We run a tight ship here. Clockwork precision.

ALICE 1030. Sleep Time.

VICTORIA Exactly. It is now 1032.

ALICE 1100 Music. Piano. Suzuki Method.

1130 Dance. Classical. Nijinksy.

1200 Drama. Non Textual. Boal.

1230 Art. Post Modern. Warhol.

1300 Wellbeing. Babygolates…

Babygo…what??

VICTORIA Babygolates. You've heard of Pilates? Babygolates is my 'baby' so to speak. Very popular with the parents. Now, I am going to count our earnings and check the share price. You've got 27 minutes to have this place spic and span. Get to it!

She returns to her lookout. REBECCA dutifully obeys. ALICE less so.

ALICE This is no life…

REBECCA Sssh!

They scrub the floor.

ALICE *[to herself]* I've got to do something.

Excuse me?

She waves to VICTORIA.

VICTORIA What is it now?

ALICE Where's the bathroom?

VICTORIA   It's not time…

ALICE   Yes but…

She crosses her legs.

VICTORIA   Oh all right. Just this once. Rebecca! Show her the lavatory.

ALICE grabs REBECCA's hand.

VICTORIA   And don't take all day!

REBECCA and ALICE exit.

VICTORIA listens.

Sound of a tap running.

VICTORIA   Don't waste water!

Toilet flushes.

End scene.

scene eight

1. Why is she called Miss Victoria? Is this a character clue? If so, can you work out who she is referencing?
2. How has the way we care for our children changed over time?
3. How has parenthood changed? What sorts of pressures are on parents today that might be relatively new?
4. Is child care a replacement or substitute for family? How old do you think children should be when they go into child care?
5. In what way is Rebecca different to Alice?
6. What is satire? How do we use satire?
7. Consider whether you think there is a specifically Australian sense of humour. Where does it come from? Does it ever get us into trouble? For instance, Australian troops are famous for laughing in the face of adversity and making fun of terrible situations like those encountered at Gallipoli. Indigenous Australian humour often makes light of terrible situations as a means of survival. Irish humour often does the same. In pairs, see whether you can think of any recent examples of this kind of humour.

Playing characters that aren't the same age as we are is part of the fun and challenge of performing. All we need to do is discover the essence of a character. For example, if asked to play an old person we might simply focus on moving more slowly.

- Research the Victorian era. Collect images and information about life in Victorian England.
- Stand in a circle in a 'neutral' position. Slowly change your position so that you discover the essence of a baby. This doesn't mean just sucking your thumb! Use your whole body. Return to neutral and explore different stages

of life. Finish with old age. Remember you're not trying to mimic these stages but discover their essence.

- Design costumes for this scene. Find examples (swatches) of the different types of fabric they might wear.
- Make a list of props for this scene. Draw them. What would you make them out of?

References

The 7 Stages of Grieving (an Australian play by Wesley Enoch and Deborah Mailman)

The Adventures of Priscilla, Queen of the Desert (1994 Australian film)

'All the world's a stage …' (the seven stages of man monologue from Shakespeare's comedy *As You Like It*)

Angela's Ashes (1996 memoir by Irish author Frank McCourt)

Babakieuria or Barbeque Area (1986 ABC TV satire of black–white relations)

Gallipoli (1981 Australian film)

Muriel's Wedding (1994 Australian film)

scene nine

A fun park.

ALICE and REBECCA slide down a storm-water drain that the CAST create. It is like a slippery dip. They laugh and scream with delight.

They land at the entrance to a Fun Park. Inside there are various Pavilions and Stalls like at the Easter Show.

The surrounds are heavily polluted.

ALICE	Free!
REBECCA	Where are we?
ALICE	Who knows?

REBECCA shields her eyes.

REBECCA	Very bright.
ALICE	You'll get used to it.
REBECCA	That was so fun.
ALICE	Good.

REBECCA looks around. She hasn't been outdoors for years.

REBECCA	Wow.
ALICE	Look at that!
REBECCA	It's so…so…open.
ALICE	All that ends up in the sea.
REBECCA	I'm…
ALICE	We should clean it up.

She starts picking up rubbish.

REBECCA	I'm not sure about this.
ALICE	People!

She realises REBECCA is freaking out.

ALICE You ok?

REBECCA We better get back.

ALICE Don't be silly.

REBECCA She'll kill me.

ALICE She's your past.

ALICE takes REBECCA'S hand.

REBECCA You don't get it.

ALICE There's a whole world out there.

REBECCA Not for me there isn't.

ALICE There is now.

ALICE tries to lead REBECCA off. She resists.

REBECCA Don't.

She folds her arms.

ALICE What?

REBECCA It's all right for you.

ALICE You're behaving like a child.

REBECCA ignores her.

ALICE Oh come on. We're not going to get anywhere…hey! This is crazy. What? What?? Don't just stand there with that…that look on your face.

REBECCA Whatever.

ALICE Hey. I'm talking to you. Don't ignore me. I said don't ignore me.

REBECCA ignores her.

ALICE Oh right. Two can play at that game. I'm not talking to you then. I'm not. Did you hear me? I'm not talking to you!

scene nine

ALICE folds her arms and waits, and waits and waits!

ALICE This is pathetic. Hello? Oh look, come on. Ok. You win. I'm sorry.
REBECCA Pardon?
ALICE I said I'm sorry.
REBECCA You what?
ALICE I was insensitive.
REBECCA You said sorry.
ALICE I did.
REBECCA Wow.
ALICE I know how hard it is.
REBECCA I've never done anything like this.
ALICE Me either.
REBECCA For real?
ALICE I know where you're coming from.
REBECCA You do?
ALICE I think so. I'm not very good at this…this friendship thing.
REBECCA Me either.
ALICE Let's see what we can see.
REBECCA Ok…

ALICE points to the Fun Park.

ALICE I'm game if you are.
REBECCA What is it?
ALICE 'Fun Park'. Check it out?
REBECCA Should we?
ALICE I'm up for it if you are.
REBECCA You won't abandon me?

ALICE   No.
REBECCA   Promise.
ALICE   I promise…

ALICE peers at her name tag.

ALICE   …Rebecca.
REBECCA   Can I ask you a favour?
ALICE   Sure.
REBECCA   Call me Beck.
ALICE   Beck?
REBECCA   I hate Rebecca.
ALICE   Shall we?

They link arms and skip into the Fun Park.

This is an almost surreal world. Life is lived vicariously through technology.

They enter the Games Pavilion. Games are 'played' on gadgets. There could be all sorts of sports being played here.

A BOY is playing a type of GameBoy. TWO WARRIORS crouch as if waiting for the starting pistol. The BOY punches the controls, bringing the WARRIORS to life. They fight – a stylised, Kung Fu kind of battle with appropriate sound effects. It becomes increasingly violent.

ALICE and REBECCA try to stop the fight.

BOY   What are you doing?
ALICE   This is out of control.
BOY   I know. Cool isn't it?
ALICE   No.
BOY   You want me to turn them on you?

scene nine

He presses the GameBoy. The WARRIORS turn slowly to face ALICE and REBECCA.

REBECCA   I don't like the look of this.

ALICE   Me either. Let's get out of here.

They escape this ugly scene and come to a Chat Room.

An OLD MAN, a HOUSEWIFE and a NICE GIRL type as they speak.

OLD MAN   Hi there.

HOUSEWIFE   Hello

OLD MAN   What's goin' down?

HOUSEWIFE   I've got so much to do. I can't tell you how busy I am. I never seem to get a moment to myself. Openings every night of the week! I'm so in demand.

OLD MAN   You oughta come down the beach. I just had the maddest surf. Like you wouldn't believe the waves. They're huge man!

HOUSEWIFE   Hang on a tic. I'll tell the limo to wait. You want my address? I don't want to seem like I'm brushing you.

OLD MAN   Sure!

HOUSEWIFE   sexyfungirldotcom.

She returns to her housework. The OLD MAN types.

OLD MAN   Hey, how're you doin'?

NICE GIRL   Oh…you know…pretty black.

OLD MAN   Wanna hang out?

NICE GIRL   Oh man, I'm so like intense. You know?

OLD MAN   Wow!

NICE GIRL   Yeah. Like I dunno. Everyone's always hassling me, you know? I don't need all these friends. Like why am I so popular?

OLD MAN	Unreal. I'd so like to get to know you.
NICE GIRL	Everyone does.
OLD MAN	What's your email address?
NICE GIRL	darkgothdotcom. What's yours?
OLD MAN	sexysurferdudedotcom.
REBECCA	They're full of it.
ALICE	Why do they have to pretend to be something they're not?

They leave.

REBECCA	Look!

The Family Pavilion.

ALICE	This looks more like it.
REBECCA	Can we?
ALICE	Why not?
REBECCA	I've always wanted a family.

They enter.

A DAUGHTER is 'talking' to her MOTHER. The MOTHER is having coffee with friends.

MOTHER	Hello darling!
DAUGHTER	Oh…hi Mum!
MOTHER	Everything ok?
DAUGHTER	Great.
MOTHER	Good. Better go.
DAUGHTER	Bye Mum.
MOTHER	Love you!
DAUGHTER	You too!

The MOTHER returns to her coffee. The DAUGHTER is distraught.

They freeze.

ALICE and REBECCA move on to another scenario.

A DAD is on the golf course. He talks to his SON.

DAD	Hello?
SON	Dad.
DAD	Hi there Tiger! Hey…what's up? You look a bit worse for wear.
SON	Do I?
DAD	Yes.
SON	Oh I…
DAD	Let me have a look at you. Come closer.
SON	I'm ok Dad.
DAD	Your eyes, they're bloodshot.
SON	Are they?
DAD	Yes. God son! This is no good. This is no good at all.
SON	I'm just a bit…
DAD	What the hell is going on here?
SON	Nothing…
DAD	You look bloody awful.
SON	Do I?
DAD	This is the limit!
SON	No Dad…
DAD	I won't stand for this.
SON	Don't….

DAD	You're burning yourself out. You're working too hard. You need a break. You need to look after yourself. God son! This is terrible. It's only a bloody exam for God's sake! There's no need… Tell you what mate, I'll put a few extra dollars in your kick to tide you over. Reward for your hard work.
SON	Thanks Dad.
DAD	I am your father.

A SISTER joins the conversation.

SISTER	You're mine too Dad!
DAD	Better go…hang on…play through guys!

He gestures to GOLFERS.

SISTER	Sorry to bother you!
DAD	Come on sweetie pie! Don't be like that … hold on! What is it about you? You look so different. God. You've grown into a young woman before my eyes. It's incredible. Last time I looked you were a little girl, my little girl, now you're a blossoming little…
SISTER	Don't say it Dad…
DAD	Fruit tree.
SISTER	God!
DAD	Ok. Better fly.

ALICE and REBECCA explode.

ALICE	Hey!
REBECCA	Come back!
ALICE	You can't do that!
REBECCA	Hey! Hey!

ALICE runs around the other Pavilions shouting.

scene nine

ALICE — Guys! Guys! You gotta get a life. This place is killing you.

Everyone stares at her as though she's mad.

ALICE — This is no life.

TWO GUARDS approach them.

GUARD 1 — What have we here then?
ALICE — This is crazy.
GUARD 2 — Don't you dare!
GUARD 1 — That tone of voice.
GUARD 2 — A bit of respect.
REBECCA — Who are you?
GUARD 1 — Public nuisance?
GUARD 2 — Creating a disturbance?
ALICE — What sort of a place is this?
REBECCA — It's a nightmare.
GUARD 1 — Challenging authority.
GUARD 2 — Not obeying rules.
REBECCA — Don't be stupid.
GUARD 1 — Disrespect.
GUARD 2 — Insolence.
GUARD 1 — Arrest them?
GUARD 2 — My pleasure.
ALICE — You can't arrest us.

The GUARDS arrest them.

GUARD 1 — We just did!

End scene.

scene nine

Discussion points

1. What do you think of the recurring image of sliding down a drain? Where do you think that comes from? What does it suggest?
2. Why is the 'Fun Park' polluted?
3. What sorts of things cause conflict in relationships? Is friendship unconditional? Can people argue and still be friends?
4. How do you build trust with other people?
5. What is the basis of friendship?
6. How has the internet affected the way we relate to each other?
7. Are there any dangers associated with Facebook, Twitter and sending text messages?
8. How long do you think images last on the internet?
9. What is Surrealism? What is surreal about this scene?
10. What elements of this scene might resemble Lewis Carroll's *Alice's Adventures in Wonderland*?

Activities

In contemporary theatre making we have to embrace the world around us. We might use multimedia and computers. Whatever we do has to connect with a contemporary audience. That's you.

- Find images of heavily polluted environments. Use them to create the world of this scene. This might be by projected images or you might build props that the performers bring on stage.
- Complete some trust exercises. Stand in a circle. Someone stands in the middle. The circle needs to be close enough so that you can gently push the person in the middle to and fro. Lead each other around the school. One person wears a blindfold; the other leads. There are lots of trust exercises you can try.

scene nine

- Create frozen images to represent the characters in the 'Fun Park'. Start with a neutral position and then sculpt each other into the adult characters. You might create someone playing golf whilst talking on a mobile. Or a mother talking to a daughter.
- Use multimedia to create a sense of modern communication. For instance, conversation is typed on to a keyboard. The words are projected onto a screen. The characters never have physical contact with each other. Nor do they look at each other. They read the words on the screen, then reply.

References
Coney Island (Brooklyn, New York)

The Last Picture Show (a 1971 coming-of-age film)

Luna Park (Melbourne and Sydney)

scene ten

A courtroom.

The tribunal sits. The JUDGE presides over the tribunal. REBECCA and ALICE are in the 'dock'.

PROSECUTOR The Defendant stands charged with 'Threatening the Status Quo'. She has a record of subversive activity. Your Honour, the Defendant needs to be made an example of to preserve the rightful order of things. If she is allowed to escape sentencing we will be sending the wrong signal to those of her ilk. In these difficult times we must be vigilant. We must root out those who seek to undermine the moral fibre of this Great Country of ours. We must be on guard 24/7. We must be prepared to do whatever it takes to preserve the sanctity of our way of life.

Sits.

JUDGE Thank you my Learned Friend. Very salient words. Very salient indeed. I now call on the Defence to present their case. If they have one. The Defence? Is there no Defence?

PROSECUTOR I rest my case Your Honour. Who can defend the indefensible?

ALICE I can!

JUDGE I beg your pardon?

ALICE I'll defend Beck.

JUDGE You are a child.

ALICE If I'm old enough to be charged I'm old enough to offer a defence.

JUDGE But are you qualified?

ALICE I'm Beck's friend!

REBECCA	Go Alice.
JUDGE	Can you speak the Queen's English?
REBECCA	What's that?
ALICE	I can make sense, which is more than he does.
REBECCA	Good one!
JUDGE	Order!
ALICE	You can't arrest someone for being a teenager.
JUDGE	I'll be the judge of that.
REBECCA	What are we charged with then?
JUDGE	You heard.
ALICE	Tell us?
JUDGE	Show some respect.
REBECCA	Why?
JUDGE	Why? Why do you think? We're adults and you are children, that's why.
REBECCA	You're a bunch of ignorant dickheads that's what you are!

OFFICIALS spring to life.

OFFICIAL	She swore.
OFFICIAL	We'll send her to her room.
OFFICIAL	We'll ground her until it suits us for her to go out.
OFFICIAL	We'll give her a long and boring sermon on her responsibilities and her lack of respect for the older generation.
OFFICIAL	We'll get really drunk and behave like complete morons and pretend it never happened.
OFFICIAL	We'll carry on as though we never did any of the things they are doing.
PROSECUTOR	Your Honour this insurgency must be nipped in the bud.

scene ten

OFFICIAL	We must send a clear message.
OFFICIAL	We cannot be weak.
OFFICIAL	We must set an example.
JUDGE	Bring forward the Defendant.
ALICE	This is absurd. It is a beat up. We haven't done anything wrong.
JUDGE	Speak when you are spoken to young lady. Do you have anything to say?
ALICE	What about?
PROSECUTOR	I rest my case Your Honour.
OFFICIAL	Well put.
OFFICIAL	Telling blow.
OFFICIAL	Sealed the deal.
ALICE	You're all mad.
REBECCA	This is bullshit!
PROSECUTOR	Contempt of Court!
REBECCA	Contempt's the word!
JUDGE	How do you plead?
ALICE	We're not buying into this.
JUDGE	You are pleading guilty?
REBECCA	She is not pleading guilty!!
JUDGE	I'll be the judge of that!
PROSECUTOR	Your Honour, I suggest the Tribunal be called on to pass their Verdict. There being no more to add to what is, after all, an open and shut case we should get this out of the way and retire for a long and very expensive lunch at one of Sydney's most pretentious restaurants.
JUDGE	An outstanding summation.
ALICE	You ought to be ashamed of yourselves, you have perverted our Criminal Justice system.

OFFICIAL	Who does she think she is?
OFFICIAL	An elite?
OFFICIAL	An 'intellectual'?
OFFICIAL	A bleeding heart!
ALICE	In a true democracy the innocent are innocent until proven guilty.
OFFICIAL	You're not just a pretty face!
JUDGE	The verdict?
OFFICIAL	Guilty.
OFFICIAL	Guilty.
OFFICIAL	Guilty.
OFFICIAL	Guilty.
OFFICIAL	Guilty.
OFFICIAL	Guilty.
ALICE	Innocent.
OFFICIAL	Innocent.
JUDGE	I sentence…I …what did you say? Innocent?
OFFICIAL	Innocent.
JUDGE	Whaaattt?
OFFICIAL	Innoc…Guilty!
REBECCA	How can she be guilty?
PROSECUTOR	Because we say so you stupid little girl!
REBECCA	Don't call me stupid, you pompous old fart!
JUDGE	By a unanimous decision of this Court I declare the Defendant Guilty as charged.
ALL	Guilty as charged! Guilty as charged! Guilty! Guilty! Guilty as charged!
ALICE	This is a bloody disgrace!
OFFICIAL	Fifty lashes.

scene ten

OFFICIAL	String her up by her toenails.
OFFICIAL	Hang her from the rafters.
OFFICIAL	Cut out her gizzards
OFFICIAL	Put her on the rack.
OFFICIAL	Deport her.
JUDGE	Good idea. I hereby sentence you to immediate Deportation. You have three minutes to leave.
OFFICIAL	Put them on a leaky boat.
OFFICIAL	Send them back to where they came from.
REBECCA	No. Please. No.
ALICE	You can't. You don't understand.
JUDGE	I'll let you into a little secret sweetie, I can do whatever I like!
ALICE	Beck's life was torture.
OFFICIAL	All stand.
JUDGE	Time starts now.
REBECCA	I'm begging you.
ALICE	This isn't fair.
PROSECUTOR	Read about it in the papers. You lost. We won.
JUDGE	Two minutes fifty five seconds.
ALL	We're coming to take you home ha! ha! We're coming to take you home.
ALICE	We've only got one chance.
REBECCA	Bathroom?
ALICE	A tunnel of possibilities?
REBECCA	We need to go to the toilet!

End scene.

- Compare the Australian justice system to the justice systems of a number of other countries.
- Make a list of punishments meted out to offenders in the early days of settlement in Australia.

References

The Bill of Rights (US)

The Constitution of Australia

The Female Eunuch (1970 book by Australian Germaine Greer)

'I Am Woman' (1972 song by Helen Reddy)

Law & Justice (http://www.australia.gov.au/topics/law-and-justice)

'Sisters Are Doin' it For Themselves' (1985 duet by The Eurythmics and Aretha Franklin)

'Stupid Girl' (2006 song by Pink)

Trial By Jury (comic opera by Gilbert and Sullivan)

scene eleven

The coast.

Moonlight shines on the ALBATROSS. He is covered in OIL.

ALBATROSS Flipping wings! Covered in oil. Disaster. Can't move. Bad. Very bad. How? I'm flying along, head in the clouds, ruminating. Below me, the mother of all bream. Almost taste it. Glassy sea, gentle breeze, glistening sun, perfection! Should have been wary. Should have known better. Fly blind. Choose moment. Dive, snap up prize, prepare to ascend. Preoccupied. Don't notice conditions altered. Break through water, flap wings. Pain. Wings leaden. No headway. Barely surface. Dripping oil. Fear. White fear. Sea covered with blanket of black muck. Suffocating. Bream's thrashing about. Exhausting! Not gaining altitude, tiring badly. Have to release fish. Into what? Oil. Fish drops. Hits oil. Can't move. Can't breathe. Can't live. Still. Dead. Bad death. Bad. Bad. Bad.

ALICE and REBECCA emerge from another tunnel.

ALICE Albatross!!
ALBATROSS Ghostbusters?
ALICE Ohmygod.
ALBATROSS I didn't think I was going to see you again.
ALICE Look at you. What's…oil! You're covered in it.
ALBATROSS No more squeaky joints!
REBECCA You look terrible.
ALBATROSS Too kind.
ALICE This is my friend Beck.
ALBATROSS Friend?

REBECCA	Poor old thing.
ALBATROSS	Enough of the old!
ALICE	This is terrible.
REBECCA	We gotta clean it off.

They try.

ALBATROSS	Nothing is as bad as it seems.
REBECCA	You're dripping oil.
ALBATROSS	Every cloud has a sliver lining.
REBECCA	Yeah?
ALBATROSS	A bird doesn't always get this kind of attention. I rather like it.
ALICE	We'll get you flying in no time.
ALBATROSS	You will?
REBECCA	Yep.
ALBATROSS	My feathers were my strong point. There go the endorsements. My modelling career choked by an oil slick.
ALICE	We'll get you back up there, won't we Beck?
ALBATROSS	Please, you mustn't let the other birds see me like this!
REBECCA	Don't worry.
ALBATROSS	I have my pride you know.
ALICE	Of course you do.
ALBATROSS	Is it coming off?
REBECCA	Sort of.
ALICE	We're gonna stay here till it does.
REBECCA	Sure are!
ALBATROSS	It's not is it?
ALICE	Now, don't go getting all down in the beak.

scene eleven

ALBATROSS   My wings feel so heavy.

ALICE   We're onto it.

REBECCA   Trust us.

ALICE   We'll have you back to normal in no time.

ALBATROSS   You're just humouring me.

ALICE   This is just a bit of a hiccup.

ALBATROSS   A hiccup?

ALICE   Well, put it this way, there's nothing quite like the feeling of flying through unsettled weather and coming out the other side into bright sunshine. It makes it all worthwhile.

ALBATROSS   Does it just?

ALICE   That's what an old bird taught me!

ALBATROSS   Old? Stop calling me old!

ALICE   If you stop flapping about we might be able to clean you up. Now stand still!

They clean furiously.

ALICE   You know what? We've got to do something.

REBECCA   Yeah! What?

ALICE   Something.

ALBATROSS   Good girl.

REBECCA   Who's gonna listen to us, we're just kids.

ALICE   We can't just stand by…

REBECCA   You're right.

ALBATROSS   Sounds like you guys are on a mission.

ALICE   Yeah…I think we are. Aren't we?

REBECCA   Looks like it.

ALICE   Lots of stuff needs changing.

ALBATROSS Heads pulled out of the sand?

ALICE Exactly.

ALBATROSS Get me cleaned up and I'll take you.

REBECCA Where?

ALBATROSS Wherever you need to go.

End scene.

scene eleven

Discussion points

1. Although this is one of the shortest scenes in the play it is also one of the most moving. Why do you think this is so?
2. What is it called when a character speaks directly to the audience?
3. Describe the language in this scene. How does it shape your understanding of what is happening?
4. What other famous historical characters have sacrificed themselves for the greater good?
5. Do you know who the Ghostbusters are?
6. Where does the saying 'every cloud has a silver lining' come from?
7. What is the 'turning point' in this scene?

Activities

One of the ways that theatre differs from most film and television is when a character directly addresses the audience. Shakespeare used this device in the 'soliloquy', where a character shares their innermost thoughts with the audience.

- Have everyone in the class learn and deliver some of the Albatross' monologue.
- A tableau is a frozen image. In groups, create tableaux of the images described by the Albatross.
- Workshop ways to create the 'oil' that covers the Albatross.

References

Ghostbusters (1984 film)

Oil spills and their impact on wildlife

'Pollution' (song by satirical songwriter Tom Lehrer)

scene twelve

Canberra.

The ALBATROSS flies ALICE and REBECCA over the national capital.

REBECCA	This is the maddest fun.
ALICE	Stick with me kid. Drains, tunnels, flights of fancy.

They high five.

ALBATROSS	Ok ladies. I think I can see your destination.
ALICE	Down there?
ALBATROSS	That's it.
REBECCA	It's so brown.
ALBATROSS	It's a wide brown land.
ALICE	Over there. Smoke.
ALBATROSS	Fires.
ALICE	Not very welcoming.
ALBATROSS	Now you know why I hate to come inland.
ALICE	I'm sorry. I didn't mean…
ALBATROSS	Does a bird good to go outside his comfort zone.

They 'land'.

ALBATROSS   Here we are.

ALICE and REBECCA hop off.

ALBATROSS	Over there.
ALICE	You head back, we'll find our way.
ALBATROSS	I'll wait on the lake. I'm tired. Been a big season. Off you go. You've got things to do.

He flies off.

ALICE	Come on then, let's kick some butt.
REBECCA	You go.
ALICE	Sorry?
REBECCA	This is your journey Alice.
ALICE	Yes but…
REBECCA	I want to explore a few things. Go on. I'll be fine. Now you've given me the confidence.

REBECCA hugs her.

REBECCA	Thanks Alice. Love ya.
ALICE	Love ya too.

She indicates to call. ALICE nods. REBECCA heads off.

The SPEAKER rushes on.

SPEAKER	'I'm late, I'm late, I'm late for a very important…'
ALICE	Excuse me.
SPEAKER	Just warming up the vocal chords!
ALICE	I'm looking for…
SPEAKER	Curtain in five.
ALICE	Am I in time?
SPEAKER	Showtime? It's showtime all right. Indeed it is!
ALICE	I thought…
SPEAKER	Don't.
ALICE	Don't what?
SPEAKER	Don't think. Act.
ALICE	This is the national capital?
SPEAKER	This is where the heart of the nation beats. This is where the big decisions are made, where true power resides.

scene twelve

ALICE Oh God, I was looking for Parliament.

SPEAKER You've found it young lady. Welcome to the People's House. The Heart of the Nation.

They enter PARLIAMENT.

MEMBERS play games like 'Scissors, Paper, Rock' and other children's games as the SPEAKER takes his/her place.

The PM and LEADER of the OPP enter.

SPEAKER The National Anthem!

They stand. The 'Star Spangled Banner' plays. Hands on hearts. The PM sobs.

SPEAKER Hold your horses!

Music stops.

PM I love that tune…

SPEAKER Order. The National Anthem.

'God Save the Queen' plays. All spring to attention and salute.

OPP Hang about!

Music stops.

SPEAKER I thought something was amiss. Have we got…

The 'Play School' theme plays. They do a 'Play School' routine.

SPEAKER That'll do. We've got the general idea. Order! Order! Will the House be seated?

All sit except ALICE, who is left standing.

SPEAKER Yes?

They all look at ALICE.

SPEAKER You have a question?

109

ALICE	Yes, I do.
SPEAKER	With or without notice?
ALICE	I want to ask why….
SPEAKER	Ask why? Why?
ALICE	What's happening is appalling….
ALL	Hub bub hub bub.
SPEAKER	Order! I call on the Honourable Member for…which seat?
ALICE	You have to do something about it!
SPEAKER	You must have a seat. Where's your seat?
ALICE	I don't need to sit…
POLITICIAN	She can sit on me.

Those on the RIGHT laugh, the LEFT boo.

SPEAKER	You must have a seat!
PM	I wonder…
SPEAKER	The PM.
OPP	You wonder?
PM	Indeed, I wonder.
OPP	What do you wonder?
PM	I wonder is she one of us? Or is she one of them?
SPEAKER	Let's see shall we? Would the Members of the Government move to their right.

They try.

POLITICIAN	There's no room. We can't move any further to the right.
SPEAKER	I see. Will the Members for the Opposition all move to their left?

scene twelve

They freeze.

POLITICIAN   We're not going there. You know what happened last time.

SPEAKER   What about in the middle?

They all jostle for positions. They fall over each other fighting for the middle.

SPEAKER   Order! Order! This isn't a bloody chook yard.

POLITICIAN   Get out of my seat.

SPEAKER   Sit down! You're behaving like a silly old rooster.

ALL   Cock a doodle do! Cock a doodle do!

POLITICIAN   Any cock'll do!

ALL   Guffaw, guffaw, guffaw!!

SPEAKER   Order! Order! Order in the House.

They return to their seats leaving ALICE in the middle.

POLITICIAN   The middle appears to be taken!

ALICE   I'm sorry but…

SPEAKER   What did you say?

PM   Did she say sorry?

OPP   I think so.

PM   Point of order!

SPEAKER   The Prime Minister.

PM   We don't say sorry.

ALL   Hear hear.

PM   We never say sorry.

ALL   Hear hear.

SPEAKER   All those in favour?

ALL   Aye!

SPEAKER	Against?

Silence.

SPEAKER	The ayes have it. That's settled then. Any further business?
ALL	Mumble. Mumble.

Silence.

ALICE	May I speak now?
SPEAKER	Why not?
ALICE	Parliament is where laws…
SPEAKER	Good question.
ALICE	Will you stop interjecting?
POLITICIAN	Interjecting? I'll give you interjecting sweetie pie!
POLITICIAN	Dickhead!

Again, the RIGHT laugh and the LEFT boo.

SPEAKER	Brilliant rhetoric.
ALICE	Stop behaving like a bunch of tossers and pay attention! I haven't got much time…
POLITICIAN	You've got great legs though!

The LEFT gasp.

SPEAKER	Withdraw that remark.
POLITICIAN	You've got great…
SPEAKER	Don't go there.
POLITICIAN	You've got great…great…hair!
ALL	Hear hear!
ALICE	There are matters of national and international importance that require your attention.
ALL	Hear hear!

SPEAKER	I declare the Member's motion carried.
ALICE	Be quiet! I haven't finished!
ALL	Guffaw, guffaw, guffaw.
SPEAKER	The Constitution is now amended to include the new Law.
ALICE	What new law?
POLITICIAN	Yours, brown eyes!
POLITICIAN	Don't you know the rules?
ALICE	This is impossible!
POLITICIAN	If a Member comes up with an idea, that becomes a Law until someone else comes up with a new idea and then that becomes the Law.
PM	Democracy. Our boys died for that.
OPP	And a few others too.
PM	Great system eh?
OPP	You can do anything in the name of Democracy.
ALICE	That's why I am here, to exercise my democratic right.
POLITICIAN	Of course if a poll suggests a Law may be unpopular in a marginal seat, we change it!
SPEAKER	We're cooking with gas today! Any more original thoughts?
PM	I've got an idea.
OPP	That's original!
PM	I've been inspired by my little friend here. It occurs to me that all Members of the House should wear a sock on their hand at all times.
OPP	What a bright idea.
SPEAKER	The PM's motion? All those in favour?
ALL	Aye!

SPEAKER	Against?
ALL	Nay!
SPEAKER	The Ayes have it! I declare the motion carried.

They put a sock on their hands.

ALICE	Will you stop this silly nonsense?
POLITICIAN	Why?
ALICE	You are not achieving anything of substance!
SPEAKER	Well said. I declare the Member the new Prime Minister.
PM	You Judas!
SPEAKER	I must serve the Parliament without fear or favour. We all know that whoever says anything remotely sensible becomes the Prime Minister until someone else says something sensible.
OPP	Wow.
PM	Radical.
OPP	Out there!
ALL	A vote!
ALICE	This is a madhouse.
SPEAKER	Well spoken.
ALL	Bravo.
ALICE	I have a point of…
POLITICIAN	Apply the gag.
ALL	Gag the debate! Gag the debate.

ALICE is gagged, literally. This is followed by a standing ovation.

PM	You'll make a great PM one day with such insightful observations.
OPP	You will go down in history.
PM	This sock smells.

OPP	So does this one.
PM	What'll we do?
SPEAKER	Ask the PM.
PM	Well, as the new PM hasn't been sworn in yet, I suggest all Members put their sock in front of them.
POLITICIAN	Put a sock in it!
POLITICIAN	Idiot!
POLITICIAN	Retard.
POLITICIAN	Moron.
SPEAKER	Socks off!

All take their socks off.

SPEAKER	All Members move one seat.

They do.

SPEAKER	Socks on!
POLITICIAN	Oh, that's much better.
POLITICIAN	Mine doesn't smell.
POLITICIAN	Nor does mine.
POLITICIAN	Just what we needed.
OPP	You'll go down as a great leader.
POLITICIAN	Churchillian.
POLITICIAN	Menzian.
POLITICIAN	Bushian.
POLITICIAN	Napoleon.
POLITICIAN	Does that scan?
PM	Thank you, thank you, thank you. It has been a long and arduous campaign and I wouldn't have got here without completely abandoning my family in pursuit of personal glory. I'd like to thank them personally but I

	can't remember their names and I haven't got time and frankly, I couldn't be bothered! Think not what you can do for your country but what you can do for your own self-interest…
ALL	Bravo!
PM	Wrote it myself!
OPP	You're a genius.
PM	I like to think so.
OPP	My shout!
PM	Good chap.
SPEAKER	That's what I call a day's work.
ALL	Here! Here!

ALICE throws herself on the floor and bangs her head on the floor. The SPEAKER removes her gag.

SPEAKER	Yes?
ALICE	Shut up! Shut up! Shut up!

They do.

ALICE	Do you have any idea what you're doing? You're letting everyone down. You're meant to be adults. You're meant to be leading the way. There are some terrible things going on out there and what are you doing? You think this is clever? Behaving like…like spoilt brats. That's what you are. Spoilt brats! I should know. You can't treat people like this. It's not fair. It's just not fair. You're not doing your job.
	Change the world.
	It needs it.

The lights dim.

ALICE	What's happening?

scene twelve

SPEAKER   Take a bow!

ALICE   What?

SPEAKER   Show's over.

ALICE   No but I haven't…

The SPEAKER bows and leaves her.

ALICE   I've got something to say…

The POLITICIANS leave as ALICE pleads with them.

ALICE   No! Come back. You can't let this continue. You owe it to yourselves. You owe it to your children. You can't… you can't just stand by…we have to do something… don't we?

She is left alone. She looks at the audience.

ALICE   Don't we?

End scene.

scene twelve

Discussion points

1. Why was Canberra chosen as Australia's capital city?
2. What was Canberra before it became a city?
3. What was Federation? What was different before Federation?
4. Can you spot the reference to *Alice's Adventures in Wonderland* in this scene? What is it?
5. Why do you think the Speaker says 'curtain in five'?
6. What is Hansard?
7. What does the politicians' behaviour remind you of?
8. What is rhetoric? Can you find any examples of it in this scene?
9. What do you think is meant by the reference to Judas?
10. Who were Churchill and Menzies?
11. How has modern politics changed from the politics of 1960s and before?
12. What do Alice and Rebecca have in common? Why do you think they become such good friends?

Activities

It is often said that politics is like theatre. There is a type of theatre called 'political theatre'. Even the proceedings are kind of theatrical. The main difference is that actors know they're acting.

- If you can, visit Canberra and Old Parliament House. You could even perform this scene in the Chamber of Old Parliament House.
- Try the 'sock swapping' routine.
- Find out about the Westminster System. How does it work?
- Research the terms 'left' and 'right' in relation to politics.

References

The Australian political system

crikey (http://www.crikey.com.au/)

The Dismissal (1983 Australian film)

'Do You Hear the People Sing?' (song from the musical 'Les Miserables')

Hansard

'Imagine' (1971 song by John Lennon)

'We Shall Overcome' (US protest song that became the anthem of the Civil Rights Movement)

scene thirteen

The ALBATROSS has been shot. His eyes have been pecked by crows. He is barely alive. ALICE rushes on.

ALICE Albatross!!
ALBATROSS There you are.
ALICE What am I going to do? They wouldn't take any notice of me.

The ALBATROSS hides his head from her.

ALICE What's up?
ALBATROSS I'm very tired.
ALICE You look terrible.
ALBATROSS You're full of compliments aren't you?
ALICE What is it?
ALBATROSS I was having a bit of a look around and some shooters started taking pot shots at me.
ALICE You've been shot!
ALBATROSS Afraid so.

She hugs him.

ALBATROSS That's better.

ALICE realises his eyes have been pecked.

ALICE Oh!!!
ALBATROSS It's all right.
ALICE No! No!

He turns away.

ALICE There's blood…
ALBATROSS Don't…
ALICE Your eyes…your eyes!!

ALBATROSS	Don't look.
ALICE	What's happened? Tell me! What's happened to you?
ALABTROSS	Crows. I couldn't get away. Been winged!
ALICE	Oh my God!
ALBATROSS	Don't look Alice.
ALICE	They've pecked out your eyes. You've been blinded! God!!! What kind of a place is this?
ALBATROSS	A pretty unforgiving one.
ALICE	This is my fault.
ALBATROSS	No…
ALICE	It is. I talked you into this. I forced you…
ALBATROSS	No one forces anyone to do anything.
ALICE	I'm responsible for this.
ALBATROSS	It was my choice Alice. I didn't have to fly you here.
ALICE	You're losing blood.
ALBATROSS	Yes…
ALICE	I'll be your eyes. If you can just get…
ALBATROSS	It's all right.
ALICE	I've got to…
ALBATROSS	Don't.

He summons all his strength.

ALBATROSS	When you're way up there the world looks different. It looks smaller. Everything seems to fit. You see patterns. You feel the sun on your back, you fly through the clouds. You survive stormy weather as best you can. You try and make things better by simply being yourself. Flying. Gliding. Diving. Soaring. It is an incredible gift. You never forget that. You never can.
ALICE	How can you be so calm?

scene thirteen

ALBATROSS You have that gift now.

ALICE What do you mean?

ALBATROSS I want you to fly for me.

ALICE Me?

ALBATROSS You've earnt your wings my girl. Fly as high as you can but, remember, don't fly too close to the sun. Keep an eye out. There'll always be something that needs you. Something or someone.

ALICE You've opened my eyes and now you can't see.

ALBATROSS That's the way it is and the way it should be. My eyes are gone and I need to sleep…to sleep…to sleep.

He dies.

ALICE No…no…no!! You can't….you can't leave me. What am I…

She stands alone for a moment and then looks at the ALBATROSS.

She removes his wings and puts them on.

ALICE No guts no glory?

She checks herself out.

ALICE Pretty cool eh? Oh well, don't 'spose I can hang around feeling sorry for myself. Not now. There are plenty of oceans to cross.

She tries to take off but has no luck.

ALICE Mmm. This may not be as easy as it seems. Still….

She tries again.

Finally, after much effort, she takes off.

End play.

scene thirteen

Discussion points

1. What happens at the end of the play?
2. How has Alice changed from the character we first meet in Scene 1? Give two examples.
3. What do you think the Albatross is doing at the end of the scene when he passes his wings to Alice?
4. The Albatross is attacked offstage. What famous Greek plays employed a similar theatrical device?
5. What do you think will happen to Alice now?
6. Do you think the action in the play has been a dream?

Activities

In plays, characters usually go on a journey. This can be compared to a train trip where you travel from one place to another. A character can also be said to 'travel' from one place to another. The key to this isn't necessarily about going somewhere but it is about change. A character's journey involves change. The characters in lots of plays are changed by their experiences by the end of the play. This is one way that *Alice Dreaming* differs from *Alice's Adventures in Wonderland*.

- Can you identify the similarities and differences between *Alice Dreaming* and *Alice's Adventures in Wonderland*? List them.
- Make a chart of Alice's journey. List the things that change her.
- Make a list of the things the Albatross does that change Alice.
- Draw costumes for Alice and Rebecca.
- Find images that might inspire the Design of the play. These images might be from magazines or the web. Build a portfolio of images that might effect the look of the play.

- Make a list of songs and music that might be used in a production of this play.
- Play with 'made sounds' to underscore various scene.

References

Alice's Adventures in Wonderland (Lewis Carroll)

Looking for Alibrandi (2000 Australian film)

Medea (classical Greek tragedy by Euripides)

Oedipus Rex (classical Greek tragedy by Sophocles)

Somersault (2004 Australian film)

Thirteen (2003 US film)

For EU product safety concerns, contact us at Calle de José Abascal, 56–1°, 28003 Madrid, Spain or eugpsr@cambridge.org.

www.ingramcontent.com/pod-product-compliance
Ingram Content Group UK Ltd.
Pitfield, Milton Keynes, MK11 3LW, UK
UKHW021254180426
11947UKWH00010B/767